THE SKY

NEVER

CHANGES

THE SKY NEVER CHANGES

*Testimonies
from the
Guatemalan
Labor Movement*

Thomas F. Reed
and
Karen Brandow

ILR Press

an imprint of Cornell University Press

Ithaca and London

"Soft Evidence" by Ariel Dorfman, from *Last Waltz in Santiago*, translated by
Edith Grossman with the Author, published by Viking Penguin, Inc.,
English translation copyright © Ariel Dorfman and Edith Grossman, 1988.
All rights reserved. Reprinted by permission of the author.

First published 1996 by Cornell University Press.

Number 29 in the Cornell International Industrial and
Labor Relations Report series

Library of Congress Cataloging-in-Publication Data
Reed, Thomas F.
    The sky never changes : testimonies from the Guatemalan labor
movement / Thomas F. Reed and Karen Brandow.
      p. cm. — (Cornell international industrial and labor
relations report series ; no. 29)
    Includes index.
    ISBN 0–87546–354–1 (cloth : alk. paper). — ISBN 0–87546–355–X
(pbk. : alk. paper)
    1. Labor movement—Guatemala. I. Brandow, Karen. II. Title.
III. Series : Cornell international industrial and labor relations
reports ; no. 29.
HD8146.5.R44   1996
331.88'097281—dc20   95–52508

Printed in the United States of America

♾ The paper in this book meets the minimum requirements of the
American National Standard for Information Sciences—Permanence of
Paper for Printed Library Materials, ANSI Z39.48-1984.

To all union organizers in Guatemala, and their fallen *compañeros*, whose histories are inscribed on the soul of the Guatemalan working class.

T.R.

To the courageous and warm people of Guatemala's popular movement, who, despite my country's destructive history in theirs, took me into their family and shared laughter, sorrows, and confidences. Here is another "grain of sand" for our fight.

K.B.

Soft Evidence

Ariel Dorfman

If he were dead
I'd know it.
Don't ask me how.
I'd know.

I have no proof,
no clues, no answer,
nothing that proves
or disproves.
    There's the sky,
    the same blue
    it always was.
But that's no proof.
Atrocities go on
and the sky never changes.
    There are the children.
    They're finished playing.
    Now they'll start to drink
    like a herd of wild
    horses.
    Tonight they'll be asleep
    as soon as their heads
    touch the pillow.
But who would accept that
as proof
that their father
is not dead?
The madness goes on
and children are always children.
    Well, there's a bird
    —the kind that stops
    in mid-flight
    just wings in the air
    and almost no body—

and it comes every day
at the same time
to the same flower
just like before.
That doesn't prove anything either.
Everything's the same as it was the day they took him

                                       away

as if nothing had happened
and we were just waiting
for him to come home from work.
No sign, no clue,
nothing that proves
or disproves.

But if he were dead
I'd know it.
It's as simple as that,
don't ask me how.
If you were not alive
I'd know it.

Contents

Preface

This book is a collection of ten oral histories from individuals who have been actively involved in, or deeply affected by, the struggle for labor rights in Guatemala. The chapters include testimonies from rank-and-file activists, labor organizers, union leaders, widows of assassinated/disappeared unionists, and peasant labor organizers. The stories of women and men, adults and a child, veterans of the struggle and more recent recruits, willing participants and inadvertent victims of a family member's participation in the labor movement are all included in these pages. Through these testimonies, we learn of a people's struggle to organize unions in defense of their rights, the tremendous personal costs borne by them as a result of the struggle, and their hopes for a just society free of repression.

Since the 1950s, when a democratically elected president was overthrown with the complicity of the United States government, the struggle for labor rights in Guatemala has been a hazardous endeavor. Human rights organizations such as Amnesty International and Human Rights Watch have produced numerous well-documented accounts of serious and systematic human rights abuses against labor organizers, rank-and-file activists, and union leaders. Our goal in this book is to put a human face on these accounts by providing a forum for Guatemalans to relate their stories to us, in their own words.

Readers of these oral testimonies will note both the bravery and the pain expressed by the storytellers. The reader will also note, however, the role of the labor movement in Guatemala within the broader popular struggle for human rights and democracy. Labor rights cannot exist in the absence of institutions that provide a people the opportunity to voice their goals, dreams, and aspirations in a democratic and nonviolent way. The labor movement in Guatemala, as expressed by the participants in this project, views its struggle as part of a larger battle for human rights and democracy, and each participant in this project has espoused a nonviolent approach to the struggle.

Some of the participants have requested anonymity, and they are identified by a single name (e.g., Angel); others wish to be publicly identified, and their names appear in full (e.g., Rodolfo Robles). Whether they have shared anonymously or publicly, all have put themselves at risk of reprisal or assassination by telling us their stories.

We thank the following people and organizations for their help with and support for this project:

Frances Benson, director of the ILR Press and editor-in-chief of Cornell University Press, who believed in this project and guided the editorial process with great skill and patience.

Ariel Dorfman, for graciously allowing us to reproduce his poem "Soft Evidence" and use a phrase from it as the title of this book.

The reviewers, who offered much helpful advice and encouragement.

Gladys Creelman, who transcribed the Spanish tapes.

Lois Brandow, who helped with editing, and, over an eight-year period, supported her daughter Karen's involvement in human rights work in Guatemala.

Tom Reed's former colleagues at Texas A&M University, who provided substantial financial and collegial support for this project: Mike Hitt, and the Department of Management; Kerry Cooper, and the Center for International Business Studies; the Research Committee of the College of Business Administration; and John Norris, and the International Enhancement Grants Program of the Office of International Coordination.

Burton Weisbrod and the Center for Urban Affairs and Policy Research at Northwestern University, who provided time and space for Tom Reed to work on the project while he was a visiting scholar there from 1992 through 1993.

The Master of Arts in Industrial Relations Program at Wayne State University, which provided important financial support at the final stages of the project.

And, most of all, the participants in this project, for sharing their histories with us.

T. F. R.

Detroit and Killaloe, Co. Clare, Ireland

K. B.

Washington, D.C.

Chronology of Events

April 1976 The CNUS (Comité Nacional de Unidad Sindical/National Committee of Trade Union Unity) is formed.

April 15, 1978 The CUC (Comité de Unidad Campesina/Committee of Peasant Unity) comes to public light.

May 29, 1978 The Panzos massacre occurs in the department of Alta Verapaz in which one hundred Kekchi Indians are killed by the Guatemalan military.

July 1, 1978 General Fernando Romeo Lucas García becomes president of Guatemala and heads up four years of widespread terror and repression.

January 31, 1980 Thirty-nine people are burned to death when the Guatemalan police set fire to the Spanish Embassy, which peasant and student leaders had peacefully taken over to denounce repression in the countryside.

May 1, 1980 Dozens of participants in the Workers' Day march are disappeared and killed.

June 21, 1980 Twenty-seven union leaders are kidnapped and disappeared from the offices of the CNT (Central Nacional de Trabajadores/National Workers' Central).

August 24, 1980 Seventeen unionists are disappeared from a labor education course held at Emaus, a town in the department of Escuintla.

March 23, 1982 General Efraín Ríos Montt becomes president of Guatemala after a military coup.

August 8, 1983 General Oscar Humberto Mejía Victores overthrows Ríos Montt and becomes president.

February 1984 to March 1985 Hundreds of unionists occupy the Coca-Cola bottling plant to protest the illegal plant closing; they win.

June 1984 GAM (Grupo de Apoyo Mutuo/Mutual Support Group for Families of the Disappeared) is founded.

February 1985 UNSITRAGUA (Unidad Sindical de Trabajadores de Guatemala/Unity of Guatemalan Workers) is founded as a result of organizing meetings held in the occupied Coca-Cola bottling plant.

January 14, 1986 Vinicio Cerezo, the first civilian president of Guatemala in twenty years, takes power.

June 1986 UITA (Unión Internacional de Trabajadores de Alimentos y Similares), the Guatemalan office of the IUF, the International Union of Food and Allied Workers, opens.

June 1987 to August 1988 Workers of the Lunafil thread factory occupy the plant to protest obligatory twelve-hour workshifts; they win.

November 1987 The union of workers of the Accumuladores Victor car-battery factory is legally recognized. Eleven days later the plant is illegally closed by its owners.

December 1987 The UASP (Unidad de Acción Sindical y Popular/Unity of Labor and Popular Action) is formed.

THE SKY
NEVER
CHANGES

Members of GAM at Army Day demonstration, 1987. Photo O. Lucas

Introduction

No battle is ever permanently won, just as there are no permanent defeats. In Guatemala, and elsewhere in the world, we can take nothing for granted. There will be other, more difficult battles. Let us, therefore, always keep in mind what it takes to win.

It takes unity, courage, and staying power on the front line: If the Guatemalan workers had not stood fast, international support would have been to no avail. It takes coalition building: church groups, human rights organizations, public interest and solidarity groups, as well as other unions, were our most valuable allies. It takes money, lots of it, and the ability to raise it quickly. It takes organization: without a permanent, established, tried and true proven network of solidarity and action, local struggles will be crushed and wasted. Finally, it takes internationalism: the clear understanding that the battle of one union, however small and remote from one's country, makes a difference to all workers wherever they are.

—DAN GALIN, General Secretary of the International Union of Foodworkers, commenting on the historic victory of the Guatemalan Coca-Cola Bottlers' Union in 1985

That a labor and peasant movement exists at all in Guatemala is a testimony to the persistence and bravery of the workers in that country. Their capacity to survive continuous waves of repression, both physically and emotionally, is an example for workers and other oppressed groups throughout the world.

When Guatemalans are asked to talk about their history, some begin with the flourishing Mayan civilizations of centuries ago, others with the Spanish conquest beginning in 1492, while others see the CIA-organized coup in 1954 as the turning point in creating today's Guatemala. Workers' and peasant movements have experienced a series of growth periods, followed by intense periods of repression.

Modern labor history could begin around the decade of the 1920s. The first guilds and unions were formed then, among craftspeople and railroad, banana, and port workers. A national Department of Labor was created in 1925, but restrictions were placed on striking workers. After the Russian Revolution, workers were influenced to some degree by communist ideology.

Unions came under attack during the fourteen-year presidency of General Jorge Ubico, from 1930 to 1944. During that time, the words "union," "worker," "strike," and "labor rights" were outlawed from everyday vocabulary. People who used them were considered communists and were subject to severe punishment; many were jailed.

Unionism peaked during the "ten years of Guatemalan spring," 1944–54, after General Ubico was overthrown in a nonviolent uprising. The many gains won during those years included an eight-hour workday, minimum wages, regulation of child and women's labor, paid vacations, the right to organize, collective bargaining and strike power, labor courts for settling disputes, and a national social security system. The first Labor Code was instituted in 1947, and rights were extended to rural and public workers. During this period, more than five hundred unions were registered with the government, representing over 10 percent of the work force—a figure that exceeds the number of active unions today.

When President Arbenz began agrarian reform and expropriated idle land belonging to the United Fruit Company (U.S.), offering to pay the company the $1.2 million they claimed on their income tax forms that the land was worth, United Fruit demanded $16 million and began to call Arbenz a communist sympathizer. In June 1954 the CIA led a small army of "liberation forces" into Guatemala. Arbenz resigned and Colonel Carlos Castillas Armas was flown in the U.S. ambassador's plane into Guatemala and named president.

Immediately, all recognized unions were disbanded, leaders were jailed and executed, and peasant organizing was outlawed. Thousands of Guatemalans fled into exile. The CIA drew up a list of seventy thousand "political suspects," which included many unionists. By 1961, only fifty unions were registered. Unions were prohibited from participating in politics, and justifications for striking were severely limited.

It is important to recognize that all of this repression took place before the Guatemalan guerrilla movement began in 1962. Repression is not simply a "response to insurgency" as is often claimed by the Guatemalan army.

Unionism began to increase again in the 1970s as a result of increased industrialization in Guatemala. Peasant organizing also flourished under the impetus of the Christian Democratic Party and the Catholic church, which organized cooperatives in an effort to stave off demands for more radical change. The CUC, Committee of Peasant Unity, led a month-long strike involving tens of thousands of workers and won a wage increase.[1] Movement growth was also spurred by the 1976 earthquake, in which thousands of Guatemalans were killed, as relief efforts created opportunities for organizing which moved beyond relief and into political consciousness raising. Repression against this growth had already begun (for example, with the Panzos massacre in 1978 in which one hundred indigenous civilians were killed for organizing), but it became state policy with the Sandinista triumph in Nicaragua and the strengthened guerrilla movements in El Salvador and Guatemala. The Guatemalan army was determined not to let a similar triumph occur within its borders, and thus began a widespread campaign of selective repression in the city and wholesale massacres in the countryside.

Through a series of incidents in 1980 alone, which included the burning of the Spanish embassy during a peasant protest, repression during the International Workers Day march on May 1, and the mass disappearance of forty-four union leaders on June 21 and

1. The CUC (*Comité de Unidad Campesina*) is a grassroots organization that came to public light in 1978. Members struggle for improved working and living conditions for the peasant population.

August 24, the movement was left, as unionists themselves describe it, "with its head cut off." Labor leaders, labor lawyers, professors at the state university, and rank-and-file unionists were disappeared, assassinated, and forced into exile on a daily basis. Workers describe the dread with which they opened each day's newspapers, waiting to see who the latest victims had been. At the same time, the Guatemalan army was carrying out a scorched-earth policy in the countryside that wiped out 440 villages.

Thus, Guatemala became known as one of the worst violators of human rights in the hemisphere. Statistics indicate that over one hundred thousand citizens were assassinated, forty-five thousand were disappeared, 1 million were internally displaced, and another fifty thousand became refugees in neighboring southern Mexico.[2] In real terms, one of every nine citizens in the country was directly victimized by the repression. Then–U.S. president Jimmy Carter cut off military aid to Guatemala as a result, but that aid was quickly rerouted through other countries.

Through all of these periods of growth and subsequent repression, a few survivors always manage to wait a prudent amount of time, begin to gather clandestinely with others, and fight for increased space when the national or international climate allows for some opening. Such was the case in the 1980s. In June 1984, families of the disappeared announced the formation of the Grupo de Apoyo Mutuo (GAM), a mutual support group of relatives of the disappeared, who had met while searching for their loved ones in prisons, hospitals, morgues, and army bases.[3] They broke the silence and began strongly to criticize military repression, demanding that their loved ones be "returned alive, as they were taken away alive."

2. To be "disappeared" is to be forcibly removed from one's daily existence, to be detained and never heard from again. People have been disappeared from demonstrations, workplaces, cars, their homes, even hospital beds. The perpetrators are never found, tried, or punished. The families of Guatemala's forty-five thousand disappeared are left wondering if they will ever see their relatives again, never having the resolution of a burial or a gravesite to visit. Ariel Dorfman's poem on page vii expresses some of the feelings that arise as a result of disappearances.

3. The GAM (Grupo de Apoyo Mutuo), or the Mutual Support Group, is an organization that coordinates families of the disappeared in united efforts to obtain information about the whereabouts and fates of their relatives, as well as trial and punishment for those responsible for the disappearances and assassinations.

A few months earlier, on February 17, unionists of the Coca-Cola bottling plant found out that owners planned to shut down the plant the next day. They mobilized the workers, and by the next day more than five hundred people had come to the factory to find out what was happening. And so began a thirteen-month occupation of the plant. Rodolfo Robles, who was the secretary general of the union, led the workers to an important victory, and the factory remained open.

There were several important outcomes of this historic occupation. For the first time, the Guatemalan labor movement received international attention and support, through the help of the International Union of Food and Allied Workers. While much attention was being placed on the struggles in El Salvador and Nicaragua, Guatemala was virtually ignored, except by a small group of committed U.S. activists who had been affected themselves by the period of intense repression. Second, the physical and psychological space provided by the plant occupation allowed labor movement leaders and activists to come together in safety and begin strategizing about the movement's revival. Out of these discussions UNSITRAGUA was formed, the Unity of Guatemalan Workers, making its first public appearance in February 1984.[4] Finally, many Guatemalan organizations united in their material and political support of the plant occupiers, creating links that would last after the occupation had ended.

Internationally, Guatemala's poor human rights record had resulted in political and economic isolation. The Guatemalan military and business class recognized the need for a "facelift" to rejoin global markets and to receive aid. A decision was made to hold elections and promote a civilian president who would signal "the coming of democracy" to Guatemala, while allowing the real power behind the throne to remain in the hands of the army. The chosen candidate was Vinicio Cerezo Arévalo, who preferred to be called "Vinicio" by the general population. His election created widespread hopes among citizens that the worst was over, and there was talk of picking up where Guatemala's interrupted springtime (1944–54) had left off.

4. The UNSITRAGUA (Unión Sindical de Trabajadores de Guatemala), or Unity of Guatemalan Workers, was founded in 1985. It is a progressive central labor organization of public and private sector workers.

Soon after he took office, however, it was evident that the hopes raised by his election were ill founded. In his book on the accomplishments and failings of the Cerezo administration regarding labor, James Goldston states that "far from bringing about needed reforms to enhance the security, liberty, and welfare of working people, the military-backed Christian Democratic government has presided over a continuation of physical attacks and economic reprisals against workers who demand improved wages, safe working conditions and recognition of associational rights."[5] Two military coup attempts (1988 and 1989) pushed Cerezo's agenda even further to the right, as the army used the coups to ensure their control over how far the "democratic opening" would be allowed to grow. Many of the interviews in this book reflect the struggles of unionism during the Cerezo administration.

Along with political repression, Guatemala's declining economic situation has made it a difficult place to organize workers. It has some of the worst statistical indicators in the western hemisphere. When Vinicio Cerezo took power in 1986, sixty-five percent of the Guatemalan population was living in poverty; that percentage has risen to 87 percent, according to government statistics. This means that only 15 percent of the population has access to health care, less than half of households have running water and latrines, social welfare programs reach only 0.2 percent of the population, illiteracy is at 67 percent, and Guatemala has the worst infant mortality rate in Central America.

One cause of this situation is land distribution. According to a 1982 study by the Agency for International Development (AID), Guatemala is the worst off of all Latin America. Approximately 65 percent of the arable land is owned by 2 percent of the population of Guatemala, and land is the country's greatest generator of wealth. Nearly half a million peasants have no land. A handful of families controls the production of cotton, sugar, coffee, and beef.

Wages in Guatemala are extremely low. The minimum wage in the countryside at the time the interviews for this book were carried out was Q3.20 per day, equal to about 85 cents. According to the Guatemalan Labor Ministry, 50 percent of current landowners

5. James A. Goldston, *Shattered Hope: Guatemalan Workers and the Promise of Democracy*, Westview Special Studies on Latin America and the Caribbean (Boulder, Colo: Westview Press, 1989).

do not pay the minimum wage of Q14.50, or $2.80, a day. City workers fare slightly better, earning about $1.10 a day in 1990, now $2.80 a day. This is one of the reasons U.S. firms are closing shop and moving to Guatemala, since their profits soar when their workers can be paid so little. When inflation is taken into account, real wages declined twenty-six percent between 1980 and 1988.

Those wages only apply to people working in the formal sector of the economy. At least 50 percent of the population is unemployed or underemployed. And recent years have seen a booming of the informal economy, where people work at whatever they can find, often selling things out on the street.

A third factor affecting poverty in Guatemala is the tax system, which is the most inequitable in the entire hemisphere after Haiti's. Every attempt by Guatemalan presidents to institute tax reform (or even talk about it) has been quickly followed by coup rumors. There is a high degree of tax evasion by exporters, business owners, and landowners. Most of Guatemala's taxes are collected from the poorer classes through an "added value tax" placed on consumer products.

All these factors have combined to severely limit union activity. Estimates are that less than 3 percent of the Guatemalan workforce is organized. Of those working in the formal sector, 60 percent is engaged in the agricultural sector, since industrial development is rather limited. Many agricultural workers emigrate to the large southern coastal plantations during harvest season for temporary work, making organizing even harder. As growers turn away from traditional crops (coffee, cotton, sugar, and bananas) toward non-traditional cash crops such as snow peas and strawberries, there is less work for the peasant population. The ranks of the unionized have been enlarged, however, since a 1986 decree allowed public sector workers to organize.

The interviewees in this book explain through personal experience many of the tactics used to break up organizing efforts; they come as no surprise to those acquainted with labor studies. Managers and owners bribe, threaten, and illegally fire workers who start to organize. They illegally close their operations and open elsewhere.

Managers have begun to hire gang members, death squads, and private police forces to kidnap, drug, interrogate, and even assassinate workers. Others take a softer tack by bringing in an owner-sponsored parallel organization, called a "solidarity association," meant to prevent or supplant formation of an independent union. Even for those workers who support organizing efforts, the threat of losing a job in the country's weak economy is enough to keep many people away.

If workers do get to the stage of submitting the required paperwork for legal recognition as a union to the Ministry of Labor, or of bringing suit against an employer, they encounter another set of obstacles. The paperwork is delayed far beyond the time limits set by the Labor Code; owners bribe labor inspectors and judges to make decisions in their favor; and cases drag on for months and sometimes years. Poor workers cannot wait that long.

If all else fails, the National Police or army can be brought in to reinstate "law and order" on an occupied plantation or take over operations of a public service, leaving workers angry yet intimidated, as the memories of the last wave of repression are too fresh to be easily forgotten. Military control in the countryside makes organizing agricultural workers particularly difficult. Death threats against labor and peasant leaders have become so commonplace that they no longer pay much attention and often don't even present a formal denunciation to the police and the press.

Perhaps the most serious problem affecting Guatemala is summed up in one word that has become the focus of much attention in the popular movement and among its international supporters: impunity. Laws are not enforced, those who break the law and violate rights are rarely sanctioned, and the message is clear that there will be no price to pay for continued repression. Judges and law enforcement agents who try to do their jobs correctly are as vulnerable to threats and assassination as movement members.

The years of repression have taken their toll on the movement itself. An honest assessment uncovers power and personality conflicts, mistrust, (sometimes) false accusations of infiltration, sectarianism, and differing ideological sympathies that contribute to the challenges facing workers' efforts to unite.

Some changes in the situation of Guatemalan workers were brought about through the efforts of the U.S./Guatemala Labor Education Project (GLEP), an organization promoting solidarity between U.S. and Guatemalan workers, which was founded in 1987.

Through national campaigns against U.S. companies paying Guatemalan workers to produce goods under poor labor conditions, and through constant denunciations of labor rights violations to the U.S. trade representative under the Generalized System of Trade Preferences, GLEP has brought so much pressure to bear on the private sector that a number of helpful reforms have been made. GLEP has learned an important lesson for all solidarity workers: the need to take direction from the Guatemalans themselves. Controversy arose when a well-meaning U.S. journalist went to Guatemala and wrote an exposé about minors working under unfair conditions in factories. The uproar resulted in the firing of hundreds of young people whose families were dependent on their income for their economic survival. Similar issues are being raised by other unionists who want and appreciate the support but are unsure whether it is better to have no job than to have an exploitive, poorly paid one. Of course, the longer-term answer is to be sought by addressing the larger issue of impunity.

One might wonder why so much solidarity work is viewed with approval by such a small number of Guatemalans. Guatemalan history indicates that during its strong periods, the labor and peasant movement plays a leading role in organizing other sectors of the grassroots movement, even when it represents a statistically small part of the population. Workers have forged links with students, housewives, and settlers in marginal communities. Peasant organizers have come to recognize that they cannot deal with isolated issues of wages and working conditions without confronting the larger concerns of the demilitarization of the countryside, the welfare of those who were internally displaced by violence, and the central topic of land distribution. The majority of agricultural workers are Mayans, and the recovery of Mayan cultural values and customs has strengthened the peasant movement. A coalition of eleven sectors of Guatemala society came together in 1994 to write a series of documents and recommendations for the parties involved in negotiations to put an end to Guatemala's long civil war, and one of the topics addressed was land reform. A series of land occupations was begun in the first months of 1995, which peasants consider to be a recovery of lands stolen from them years ago.

A growing number of business people in the private sector are coming to realize that the old ways must change if they are to enter the world market as it exists today. Kidnappings and assassinations will not foster investment opportunities. Persistent labor rights violations will not gain Guatemala a secure place in the North American Free Trade Agreement, which is what much of the private sector seeks. Even if the motivations behind such changes are more self-serving than humanitarian, economic pressure has often been used to create long-lasting changes in society. The crucial question for Guatemala is whether this more "progressive" group within the private sector, and, more important, its counterpart within the Guatemalan army can prevail. For U.S. citizens, the revelations made in March 1995 concerning CIA involvement with the Guatemalan military and participation in political repression suggest that work must also be done in the United States if things are to change in Guatemala. In any event, history has shown that regardless of the actions of those who hold political, economic, or military power, Guatemalan workers, peasants, and international solidarity activists will not stop their struggle for justice.

On November 12, 1995, national elections were held in Guatemala for president and vice-president, Congress, the Central American Parliament, and local mayoral slots. For the first time since 1954, popular movement groups participated in the election process through the New Guatemala Democratic Front formed in June. Revolutionary forces and grassroots leaders encouraged citizens to vote, in contrast to previous years, when people were urged to abstain because of the corruption and meaninglessness of the electoral process. This was a test of strength for the grassroots movement, of its ability to mobilize citizens and begin to challenge traditional sectors of power on a new battleground.

Despite its newness and lack of experience, the Front surprised many people by taking fourth place among nineteen parties for the presidency and the Central American Parliament; six grassroots leaders were elected to the Guatemalan Congress. Those elected represent unions, families of the disappeared, widows, Mayan groups, and peasant organizers. This phenomenon marks a significant change in direction of the grassroots movement and in the content and style of public politics for the years to come. Movement concerns will be more difficult to dismiss as "subversive" and marginal, and the traditional political arena must now be shared with interests that represent the majority of Guatemala's poor and oppressed population. Hope remains for a new Guatemala.

Methodology

In 1990, Tom Reed wrote to Karen Brandow, who was then working with Guatemalan unionists in exile in Mexico City. Karen had spent four years living and working in Guatemala with families of the disappeared and with the labor and peasant movement; Tom had written about union organizers and union organizing in the United States, and in the early 1980s had spent a summer working with Guatemalan refugees in Honduras. A collaborative partnership was born, an interview questionnaire was written, and potential interviewees were identified through Karen's labor contacts in and outside Guatemala. We made efforts to pick a representative sampling with regard to age, race, position, history within the movement, and gender. The last was the most difficult, because at that point there were few women unionists. According to the women's group Tierra Viva, women comprised only 9 percent of the labor movement. This began to change with the growth of the *maquila*, or drawback assembly factories, which became a priority for union organizing around 1992 and whose workforce is primarily female.[6] Many other women unionists before that time were professionals, including social service and bank workers and teachers.

Once interviewees were identified, Karen contacted them about their possible participation in this project. Karen and Tom went to Guatemala in 1990 and taped interviews that varied from two to four hours in length. All participants signed consent forms and indicated whether or not they wished to be identified in the book. For those who did not wish to be, we have removed all possible identifying references from the transcript. The interviews were

6. "Drawback assembly," or *maquila*, refers to an increasingly common form of production in which components of an item (such as clothing, computers, or appliances) are shipped to businesses in a poorer country, whose low-paid workers then assemble the finished product for shipment back to the originating country. Large companies have found it profitable to assemble products in this manner, especially when governments enact favorable tax laws to encourage foreign investment and international trade. Working conditions in many *maquila* factories are notoriously bad, and workers' rights are often violated.

loosely based on the written questionnaire but were allowed to be more free-flowing and interactive, both because of the prior relationship Karen had with the participants and because it led to greater trust.

At times it was impossible to maintain an objective and "academic" stance, especially when people poured out their hearts to us and spoke of intense personal suffering, described the loss of relatives, or expressed their anger at the repressive apparatus in Guatemala. These interviews served as an opportunity for those who participated to express feelings and share previously untold stories. As we said in the Preface, our goal was to put a human face on history and statistics, to explore what made people become involved in the labor and peasant movement, how their lives had been affected, and what kept them going in the face of so much repression. The answers they gave to our questions are as varied as the interviewees themselves.

The interviewees were brought into the movement through the Catholic church, by a family member, or simply by seeing so much injustice surrounding them. They have suffered threats, loss of jobs, kidnappings, beatings, the assassination and disappearance of relatives, and exile. They have gone through periods of depression, fear, disillusionment, rage. Their strength comes from religion, from the memory of *compañeros* who have fallen over the years, and from hunger, which serves to fortify them rather than weaken them.

All the interviews were transcribed into Spanish from the tapes and then translated into English. Then began the rather arduous process of editing the translations, attempting to keep the speaker's story and language intact while making the flow more readable, and cutting out details that we considered inappropriate for public distribution.

The results are the ten interviews that make up this book, in which Guatemalan unionists and peasants speak for themselves. The importance of this cannot be overemphasized. It is a sensitive issue among many Guatemalans that anthropologists, sociologists, scientists, and journalists come to Guatemala to extract the knowledge, experience, and wealth of the people in a manner not unlike the Spanish Conquest of centuries ago. They are tired of being studied, of serving others' purposes and receiving nothing in return, of being peered at and considered "interesting" or "exotic" and then abandoned to continue their fight for justice alone.

Therefore, it is fitting that Guatemalans have a chance to speak in their own voices and that this book will be published in Spanish so that it will be more accessible to Guatemalans. As Rodolfo Robles says in his interview, "It isn't extremely important that profits be made from this book. A huge profit would be that this material return here and that people say, 'This is a portrait of me. I am that person. This is my people.' "

Nevertheless, whatever royalties result from sales of this book will be donated to the Guatemalan labor and peasant movement through the Grassroots Guatemala Program of the Network in Solidarity with the People of Guatemala (NISGUA).

This is not a book to be read quickly from cover to cover. Rather, it is designed so the reader can pick any story, read it, reflect upon it, think about how he or she would feel and behave in a similar situation, and perhaps be inspired. At the same time, we do not mean to romanticize or idealize the people portrayed in this book. They are quite human and have all the usual human traits, both positive and difficult. Some of them expose those difficulties in their stories.

We are extremely grateful to the Guatemalans who consented to participate in this project and recognize that we have been privileged to merit the trust of people who have been systematically oppressed for so long. In return for that trust we present this contribution to a greater understanding of the Guatemalan people and hope to move some readers to action through the organizations listed at the back of the book.

1

REGINALDO PAREDES

Born for Involvement

One of the longest lasting and most difficult labor conflicts in recent years was the case of the car battery factory Acumuladores Victor. This factory closed eleven days after the union received its legal recognition and reopened eight days later without a union after the owner, Victor Pasareli, "sold" his shares to his wife and changed the company's name. The thirty-three unionists at Acumuladores Victor fought a legal battle that lasted two and a half years, but they eventually gave up. Only thirteen *compañeros* remained in the conflict until the end.[1]

Reginaldo Paredes is a dedicated unionist whose faith in the legal system was shattered by this experience. He lost his job during the struggle, and it has been very difficult for him to find another one. Reginaldo started working in another battery factory but was quickly fired when he began to inform other workers about the need for health and safety standards that were lacking.

The unionists' efforts to start their own mini-factory failed when one of their machines broke down and they didn't have

---

1. *Compañeros* is a Spanish term that refers to people who are in some kind of partnership together, be it a romantic partnership, a shared political struggle, or co-workers in the same workplace. It is used in all of these senses throughout the book by different speakers and is most often used among grassroots leaders to indicate a degree of camaraderie.

the necessary funds to repair it because of a large debt they owed on other equipment.

Reginaldo worked for a long time with one of the union offices to advance the Guatemalan labor movement, but his family and economic difficulties persist. He could be a major asset to any union, yet for several years he had no workplace within which to exercise his leadership capabilities.

Reginaldo expresses no regrets for his involvement in the labor movement, and he would do the same if another opportunity presented itself. His comments on the effects of the Acumuladores Victor case are revealing: he feels that although the case was lost, other owners will be reluctant to behave in a similar manner owing to the huge costs involved in a prolonged legal process.

As a musician, Reginaldo refers several times to a protest song called "Casas de Carton," and we have included a translation of it at the end of the interview. This song expresses part of Reginaldo's motivation and commitment to labor struggles.

In the first place, I am grateful to my compañeros, Karen and Thomas, for including me in these interviews for the book you have planned. I hope the book comes to fruition and that it is a success for you and for the labor movement.

You told me that the goal of the book is to build solidarity with the Guatemalan labor movement. It should work out that way, because projects such as this can propel the labor movement ahead in essential areas, away from repression and toward economic improvements. Because of the lack of economic development in Guatemala, it's difficult for the labor movement to sustain itself. International solidarity is so important for us, because inside our country it's difficult to raise funds to sustain any movement.

We thought it was very important to speak with someone from Acumuladores Victor because of the importance of that conflict in Guatemalan labor history. Karen has known you since the conflict began in Acumuladores Victor a few years ago. But could you talk about your personal history in the labor movement? Was this the first union you joined? What led you to join the union?

Reginaldo (on left) holds up an UNSITRAGUA banner in the international Workers' Day march in Guatemala City. Photo Joe Gorin

The truth is that I began participating in the labor movement while working for Acumuladores Victor. Before that I had attended demonstrations, mostly the May Day demonstrations. I have an uncle who has been in the labor movement for many years, so I did have a guide.

I became involved in September of 1986 when we began the union in Acumuladores Victor. That was when I became conscious. Which is not to say that I wasn't conscious before then. You see, since I was little I've always liked protest songs. At that time one heard a lot of protest songs, like "Casas de Carton." So I was born for involvement.

But I didn't have the opportunity to join the movement until Acumuladores Victor. I was initiated by this union. Over time I became wiser about what pure and genuine unionism is for workers, and I continue to learn more and more.

Have you been active only in this union?

Yes, although we affiliated our union with UNSITRAGUA in 1987, so we've participated in other labor organizations or have been allied with other unions. We have been active in labor education courses in the UITA and with other compañeros in the International Federation of Metallurgy Workers, which invited us to participate because we are working in the same industry.[2] But it's impossible to discuss our participation in other labor organizations because these compañeros are not public in their union activities, and a discussion of their activities might put them at risk.

What was your level of participation in the Acumuladores Victor union when it was first being formed? When you first met Karen, you were secretary of conflicts.[3] Does that mean that you joined the executive committee of the union right away?

2. The UITA (Unión Internacional de Trabajadores de Alimientos), also known as the International Union of Foodworkers (IUF), is based in Geneva. The Guatemalan office was opened in 1986, a year after the successful settlement of the Coca-Cola workers' occupation (in which the IUF was heavily involved).
3. The secretary of conflicts, who serves on Guatemalan union committees, helps unionists settle labor conflicts that arise in the workplace.

No. At the beginning, when the union was being organized—I'll be very sincere—I didn't really want to join it. Not because I didn't want to be in the union, but because I knew most of the people, and I didn't think that they would resist when the owners acted against the union. I didn't have prior experience of my own in the labor movement, but I did know about it through my uncle. He had taught me about unions.

I knew the majority of people there in the company, and I knew I couldn't stay on the side of the owners. I'm a worker, and I have to support the compañeros who are workers. That's why I finally joined the union.

During the first six months, some compañeros were in the leadership, but they didn't know how to lead the movement. Leaders shouldn't be domineering. They should know how to act. But these compañeros wanted everything. They wanted to direct the rank and file. It can't be that way, though, because the rank and file should lead the union. The leaders are there to correct errors and to represent the union but not to act alone and to tell the workers what should be done.

That's why some compañeros were dismissed from leadership positions in the union—because of their attitudes. These dismissals hurt us, they gave the union a bad image. In the beginning, the managers were willing to talk, but these compañeros behaved in a domineering way, and that put the managers off. Then managers began to act in the same manner, or "pay with the same coins," as we say.

When one of the compañeros, the secretary of conflicts, sold out by accepting a bribe to abandon the union, I was elected to the position. Three other compañeros ran for it, but I was elected. And that's how I joined the directorate of the union in 1987, although the union had not yet been awarded legal recognition by the government.

How did the conflict emerge between the union and the company?

The conflict emerged because the owners didn't want a union. While we were organizing the union, the managers were always repressing us by accusing us of anything they could. The owner's son, who at that time was a manager, went to the extreme of hiding tools and then accusing us of stealing them. They tried to pressure us so we'd become destabilized. They did hurt our morale at times, but they never made us retreat. We continued our struggle, and on November 19, 1987, our union received legal recognition from the government.

It came out in the official newspaper that the union was legally recognized. Of course, the owners didn't like that. A week later, on Friday, November 27th, like all other weekends, we went home. We returned to work on the next Monday, the 30th, but to our surprise the door of the factory was closed. There was a note on it saying that operations had ceased and giving an address where workers could pick up their benefits pay.[4]

But according to Guatemalan law, when a company is going to fire a worker or go bankrupt, the managers must give the workers thirty days' advance notice so that they have a chance to look for other jobs. So the owners should have given us thirty days' notice, but they didn't: we came to work on Monday, and suddenly the factory was closed. And that was how the conflict arose.

We submitted all the necessary paperwork to the government that same day. We went to the Labor Inspection Office, which is where the order to reinstate us immediately should have been issued. When the labor inspectors went to the company to investigate the situation, though, there were already private police at the factory.[5] The private police didn't let us enter; they told us they weren't authorized to let anyone into the factory.

And that's how the conflict grew. Only about a month ago did it come to an end. And during all this time we were carrying out legal struggles, first in the Labor Inspection Office, then before a judge, later before the Supreme Court of Guatemala, and finally up to the Constitutional Court.

There were two rounds, two phases, of the conflict. In the first phase, we went to the labor inspectors and the judge of the first instance. Later we went to another court. Third, to the Supreme

---

4. Guatemalan labor law requires owners to set aside one month's salary for each year an employee works. This money must be given to the worker upon retirement, a layoff, or termination of employment.

5. Labor inspectors are employees of the Labor Ministry's Labor Inspection Office. Their job is to visit sites of labor conflicts, to write up reports on the incidents, and to act as mediators.

Court. And fourth, to the Constitutional Court. The Constitutional Court gave us the right to be reinstated, but the company didn't obey the order.

In the second phase, when the case went back to the first judge, the judge reversed the Constitutional Court's decision and ruled against us. We believe there was money involved here—a payoff, a bribe. He turned the road around on us. After having given us the right to be reinstated, the courts reversed the decision.

What did you think that day when you went to the factory and found the note that said no one could enter the factory? How did you feel?

Well, since I hadn't been through this before, my reaction was to place my confidence in the law. I'd read the labor laws and the Constitution, and I thought that the owners couldn't fire us because the company was served with an *emplazamiento*.[6] The owner had been notified that he couldn't take action against any of us workers, or fire us, or take any kind of reprisals against any of us. Based on this knowledge of the law, I had faith that the owners would have to reinstate us. The labor laws—the Labor Code and the Constitution—ordered it! So I didn't get overly concerned about the closing of the factory. I knew that to respect the law, the company would have to be reopened. So I wasn't too concerned.

But as time passed I learned how the laws really functioned. They were inoperable, they weren't applied as written. I can tell you that what is written in the Labor Code and in the Constitution is very beautiful, and it would be good if it were enforced. However, that's not how it is, because one thing is written there and the judges do something different. So I wasn't concerned in the beginning, but, as time passed, I began to worry, as much for my compañeros as for myself. For my compañeros because the majority of them had families: wives and children to support; rent to pay; food and school expenses; and so on. As time went on, we were unemployed and isolated from work. That was the biggest concern.

6. An *emplazamiento* is a court order, obtained by unions, that prevents a company from firing workers involved in organizing efforts. The *emplazamiento* also prevents workers from going on strike until specific points of discussion specified in the court order are resolved.

Did you discuss these things with your wife?

Yes, I did speak to her. I made her see that I couldn't abandon the compañeros and our struggle. But she didn't agree with what I was doing. She said to me, "You are getting involved in problems, and people who get involved in those problems get kidnapped and killed! They do bad things to them!"

I told her I was doing it for our children. Although I wouldn't reap the benefits of my actions, the children would reap the benefits of our struggle. But my wife said that if I were really doing it for the children, it would be better *not* to be active in the movement. "How am I going to stop supporting the workers and put myself on the side of management?" I asked her. "If you don't want to support management, to avoid problems you should quit right away, get your benefits pay, and be at peace." But that wasn't my idea. My goal was to continue to struggle up to whatever point possible, or until the end. In the end, we discovered many things. We discovered that the law is on one side: the side of the powerful.

How did your family react when you were no longer able to work because of the conflict?

Well, I can tell you that my family was against me. I couldn't talk to anyone in my family, not with my father, or my mother, or my wife because the first thing they said to me was that I should leave the job and take my benefits pay: there was no other option. I had problems with my father, and I still have them. There are differences between us. I didn't want them to insist that I give up the struggle. I told them, "I know what I'm doing. It's better to leave me alone if you don't share my opinion. It's better to leave me to do what I think is best and not to interfere in my problem because this is a personal problem. I appreciate your concern for me, but this is what I want and I can't change it." Still they keep asking me to give up on the labor movement, and to this date I have problems with my father because of this.

He wants you to quit?

Yes. One time he came to the house to pressure me to quit. I was upset because that day we had held a meeting with the business owners and their lawyer, but we hadn't come to an agreement. And more than that, in the court, and in front of an official, the company's legal adviser yelled that the owners had enough money to bribe whomever they wanted so that the workers wouldn't win their case. "And besides that," the adviser stated, "I prefer to give the money to the judges and not to you!" So that day I was already upset because of what the company's legal adviser had said to us. When I came home and my father began to talk to me about the struggle, I said to him, "Now you, too, are trying to brainwash me! It's enough that the company owners and their advisers want to do that, but now you, too?" And so we argued.

We have had our differences, and to this date we don't have the same relationship as before because the same trust doesn't exist between us. Now we're not the same, neither he with me nor me with him, particularly because he felt bad about what I had said to him. But the truth is that I never wanted to hurt him. The only thing I wanted was to make him see that I had my own ideas and they were not in agreement with his. That he should leave me in peace. He always said that suddenly something would happen to me and that they would kill me. Well, God will decide that. It's not something I'm looking for; it means that it was meant to happen.

So you haven't found much support from your family to continue the struggle?

No. The truth is, I haven't found support. In one sense I know they are right, because everyone knows you can't safely defend the interests of the workers given the attitude of the government and the owners. That's the problem that my family sees, not my being involved in the labor movement per se. They recognize that the labor movement is a good thing, but only when a person's safety is respected. This is what makes them pressure me to drop out of the struggle. They are so worried about my safety.

How many children do you have?

We have three.

And how has this situation affected the children?

Very badly. I hardly talk about this with anyone, but I'll tell you what is happening with my daughter. She was born healthy, but when she was three months old she was traumatized by problems I had with my wife. After we had argued and were so angry, my wife breast-fed the baby and the baby had a nervous reaction. So my daughter has shocks or nervous attacks now. We have taken her several places for treatment, but the doctors haven't cured her yet. We even went to a psychiatrist, and he said that the problems that my wife and I had when the baby was three or four months old traumatized her. Now my daughter has convulsions. That is the major way our family has been affected.

The doctors say that your daughter is ill because you and your wife were arguing about this problem, and that the baby realized this?

No, it's not that she got scared, but when a baby is breast-fed, the mother's bile is absorbed by the baby through the breast. The breast milk was poisoned by our arguments.

We argued because there wasn't enough money. I tried to find a way to make some, but it wasn't enough. That was when the arguments started. Almost every day there were arguments. When I came home, my wife would ask me how the conflict was going, and I couldn't lie to her. I'd say, "Maybe tomorrow will be better," and then the argument would start.

And later she became annoyed and angry. She breast-fed the baby, and that affected her to the point that now she's four years old and my daughter still doesn't walk. She only drinks from a bottle because of her illness. I didn't want to blame the arguments and breast-feeding because I couldn't really believe it. We went to the psychiatrist, and my wife talked more than I did. The psychiatrist told her that the child was suffering from all the bile she swallowed from her mother. My daughter is paying the price for my struggle.

This is what is most deeply affecting me in my home life. I don't feel free to go and work in peace because I know that at home there is a child who needs more than normal care. A normal child can be given care, and you make her well. But with my daughter, you have to give so much extra effort.

Have the doctors told you a name for your daughter's condition?

Unfortunately, we can't afford to take her to the proper place for medical care. That's the problem. We have taken her to general practitioners, but my daughter's condition needs a specialist. Some say it's epilepsy; others say that she has nervous shocks. The only thing that's certain is it started when she was four months old. She was born healthy. I can assure you that she wasn't born ill.

And have you gone to the clinic?[7]

No. But recently a delegation of compañeros from other countries came to Guatemala, and I was talking to one compañera about my daughter. She works with children with mental illness. I gave her my address, because she said that she could help me since medicine is advanced in her country. She has given me hope that they can cure my daughter there. But I haven't had the means to be able to do it. If I had the economic means, I'd send my daughter to be cured.

How have you been able to survive three years without working?

The truth is that I've sacrificed a lot. Apart from participating all this time in the labor movement, I like music. I'm in a political music group, and I'm in another commercial music group. That's where I've made some money to be able to survive, in spite of the problems with our sick daughter. My wife works and helps a little, but we're exhausted from this situation. The little that she earns isn't enough; the little that I can earn for food, for rent, for clothing for the children isn't enough.

Now I have another problem. This year my oldest daughter is studying in school, and next year my son should start school. Registering children in school is another cost. The public schools, in the long run, are like private schools because they ask for so many things that one ends up paying more in a state school than in a private school. It has been a very difficult situation. Also, the landlady keeps raising the rent, so this is a critical problem.

7. The Guatemalan office of the IUF set up a special medical clinic for unionists, workers who have been fired, and poor people in general.

You talk about how school costs are rising. Are you going to keep sending your children to school or don't you know yet?

The truth is that even if I can't afford school, I must manage because the children can't remain without the bread of knowledge. You have to realize that life goes by, and people aren't like they used to be here in our country when completing primary school was enough to get a job. Now it's not like that. Now primary school isn't even noticed. Now if you haven't studied some career, or don't have a degree, it's very difficult. Unless one grows up in the countryside, it's difficult. In one way or another I have to look for a way to send them to school so that I can leave my children something more than just their lives; at least leave them something so that they can defend themselves in the future.

Have you seen your other two children affected by this situation?

Yes, more with my seven-year-old daughter than my son. She also has been greatly affected. She has had problems because we haven't had enough money to support our family. There's a lack of vitamins and adequate diet for the children. When children are in their growing years, they need an adequate diet so they can develop without major problems from illnesses. My oldest daughter has had health problems, including anemia, from a lack of vitamins. She has a constant cough and has been sick all the time. This is something that has affected us a lot. The boy also has been ill from a lack of adequate diet and vitamins. He had a bad case of hepatitis at one time. So the labor struggle does have repercussions for my family.

Have you had problems with threats, surveillance, or other security problems?

About three or four months ago, before the conflict had ended, the company sent us letters saying that we would get our benefits pay. Soon afterward someone came looking for me at the house twice. Just one person came. Who knows if he was really alone?

The first time he came looking for me, neither my wife nor I was at home. We had left the children alone, with my older daughter in charge of the little ones. As I said, the sick one only drinks from a bottle, so we left her bottles ready and wrapped up in towels so they wouldn't get cold. My older daughter was in charge of giving the bottles to her. That day someone came to look for me. He was very well dressed with dungarees, a plaid shirt, and boots. He asked for me by name.

The landlady went out and said, "Who are you looking for?" And he gave her my complete name. "What do you want with him?" "I'm in his group," he said. "What group, he's in several," she said. "I'm a friend of his." "But what group are you in?" she insisted.

He didn't know what to say, or what the name of the musical group was. My friends who play in the band know me, and they would have named the group. The compañeros from the union would have said that they were from the union, right? This person didn't identify himself; instead, he ran away.

Fifteen days later he returned. He didn't say he was from a group. This time he said that I'd bought a pair of boots that were worth 80 quetzales,[8] but that I had given him only 40 quetzales and he wanted to talk to me. My wife thought this was strange, because in our financial situation I could buy a pair of shoes for only 20 quetzales, if at all. Why would I buy boots for 80 quetzales? "How odd, because he didn't mention anything to me about buying boots," she thought. "Yes, he has asked me for boots, but if he wants them he has to talk to me."

Then the man began to ask what time I would return home and when I had left home. My wife began to have doubts about why he was asking these questions. If he knew me, he wouldn't have had to ask so many questions. So she said, "I don't know. You can come back when he's here." And she cut him off.

So they were looking for me but never found me. More than anything they wanted to find out what time I came home in the afternoon, and that gave me something to think about. Sometimes, because of our activities, I don't get home until ten or eleven o'clock at night. When we had union assemblies, and I was the delegate to the assemblies, I would return home very late.

I began to think about my safety, and my compañeros told me that I should move. But I didn't move; I am living in the same place. I am suspicious that they were looking for me, because when

8. At the time of this interview, 80 quetzales equaled approximately 14 dollars.

my friends from the union look for me they know what time they can find me, and the people from the musical group also know when to find me.

Was this the first time that such a security problem happened to you since you became involved in the union?

No, it wasn't the first time. Another time I was followed from 11th Street to the Edificio del Centro, but that time a woman followed me. There was a time when women were used to follow people, to distract you. I realized that a woman was following me, a very elegant woman. I was able to slip away, but I realized she was following me.

How many compañeros began this conflict in November of 1987?

We were thirty-three compañeros.

And how many are left now?

There are thirteen compañeros left. Only thirteen of us have lasted until the end.

And the rest have gone to work in other places?

Because of economic pressure, they weren't able to endure the struggle. They also were pressured. They were weaker than the others and weren't able to stand the pressure.

Where have you found the strength to continue the struggle for so long, a strength that many other people haven't found?

The truth is that the conflict, the difficult situation that we are in, makes us analyze things. We are seen negatively by management, so it's going to be difficult for us to find work in another company. But if one is a traitor to the workers, one loses all options. One should always be on the side of workers, because one is never going to get anything from management. It's easier to receive support from the workers than from management. That is a fact. The workers, even if it's in small ways, always help out. They always try to find you some work, or they help to keep you going in some way. Your conscience takes hold during the conflict, and that makes you go on.

Recently you found another job. Before then, did you ever experience a moment when you thought that you couldn't go on? Did you ever think about dropping out of the struggle?

The truth is that I never stopped struggling. I had to find another job, but I didn't drop out of the labor movement. I went to my compañeros and said, "Compañeros, I have a lot of problems. I pay too much for rent. I have a lot of expenses. And I don't have any income to survive. I'm going to work, but that doesn't mean that I'm dropping out of the struggle. I will continue to communicate with you, and if there is a need for me to meet here in the afternoon with you, I'll do it."

I did get a job with a florist, making decorations. But it wasn't my destiny to work there. You see, I had been working there for two weeks and by chance one day we went to decorate at a party. I didn't feel right because we went where I didn't want to be: with the bourgeoisie, to decorate rich people's events. I felt bad, I didn't want to do that kind of work, but I couldn't find a way out of it.

People say that those who have money think they are better than others. But the owner of the shop, my new employer, was very attentive. She gave me food, breakfast and everything. She was one of the few people I could count on. One has to have some humanity, and that woman had it.

One Saturday, after we had returned from decorating a party, the woman's daughter was in the shop with us. The daughter said, "My husband is coming soon, and he is going to help us make some arrangements." "That's fine," I thought, and I didn't pay much attention to it.

I was working there, making some arrangements, when her husband came, and I saw that he was the son of the owner of Acumuladores Victor. He was Victor Pasareli's son, Ricardo Pasareli! When I saw him, I felt destroyed. I thought, "What a disgrace that this person has humiliated me!" I didn't look at him. I didn't want to see him. But he recognized me, and so I tried to act like I didn't know him. I didn't pay attention to him.

On Monday I didn't go to work. I just thanked the woman by phone. I didn't want to work there anymore. Imagine! It wasn't logical that I should leave a situation of exploitation and remain there, in a shop with the son of the owner of Acumuladores Victor. When I tried to explain this to the woman, she told me, "I am the owner here. He is my son-in-law, but he doesn't have anything to do with this business." But it wasn't logical for me to be involved with this family. It was better that he came to the shop when he did because it wasn't good for me to work there. So I was working for two weeks, and afterward I quit. I came back to the *muchachos*, to suffer once again economically.[9] However, I think quitting the shop was the best thing I could have done.

Within the political context of Guatemala, how can the labor movement continue to grow? How can the workers keep their spirits up to organize and to negotiate collective bargaining pacts?

Where there are unions, they will continue to negotiate collective bargaining pacts whenever management is not intransigent. But the question of how we can achieve greater labor participation is very important. When there is real democracy in Guatemala, and not a democracy such as exists now, the labor movement will grow. But now we have a deceitful democracy.

No, it isn't possible now to achieve major growth in the labor movement. There are organizations that exist outside the law, like Solidarismo.[10] Owners come with those organizations and offer many things. They tell the workers that they are going to be owners of the business, and that's how they fool the workers. The workers fall for it.

9. *Muchachos* literally means "boys," but Reginaldo is using the term in an affectionate way to refer to his co-workers in the factory who were illegally fired.

10. Solidarismo is a movement of management-sponsored associations designed to promote harmony and solidarity between workers and management. The ideology underlying Solidarismo is that workers and managers share the same economic and social interests; individual-based rewards and incentives are a key feature of the program. Many analysts view the solidarity movement as an anti-union strategy designed by managers to weaken existing unions and to prevent further unionization. The Solidarismo movement started in Costa Rica and came to Guatemala in 1983. There are currently several hundred solidarity associations in Guatemala.

Unfortunately the majority of workers have a low level of consciousness and respond to the highest bidder. When the time comes for a real organization of workers we come up against the fact that workers don't want to join the union because the owner treats them well. But the only thing the owner is doing is buying time, because later he turns his back on workers and sends them out into the street. The owner wins and the workers lose when this happens.

When there is real democracy, genuine democracy—and who knows when that will be—the labor movement will grow. Only if there is a radical change in Guatemala. But one should never lose hope. Faith must be maintained that sooner or later we must obtain, maybe not power—because that isn't what I think we want—but unity.

There is a lot of division between labor sectors; one central pulls for one side, and another for another side.[11] We need unity, the same objective—the defense of the interests of workers.

What hope is there now for the workers of Acumuladores Victor? What projects are you working on now?

We have several sources of hope. More than anything, there is one effort that is our greatest hope right now. There is a project, a project of being able to create our own work. I'll tell you about it, and why we are placing our hope in it.

As a result of the experience we have manufacturing batteries for cars, we would like to set up our own workshop, our own factory. But not with capitalist ends; we are sick of that. We know what that means. So we have a plan of setting up our workshop and being able to create our own jobs. It's been hard for us, because we need funds. We have asked for solidarity from compañero unionists, as well as international organizations, and some have given us help. They have helped us to set up our own workshop.

There are various objectives in this plan. I already said one objective is to create our own jobs. In the not too distant future we hope

11. A central is a representative body of various unions organized for the purposes of mutual support and cooperation on issues that cut across the jurisdiction of individual unions.

to be able to offer jobs to unemployed compañeros, workers who have gone through the same thing we have. Another objective would be that this project, when we are more established, will create a strike fund from the profits we receive.

Those are some objectives, but we have had problems apart from the economic ones that I mentioned before. This factory can't function on the street, in the open, because of what happened with the owners of Acumuladores Victor. If we put together a workshop and make it publicly known, they are going to sabotage us. Foreseeing this problem, we have promoted the proposal within labor organizations, among the compañeros who have cars. These are compañeros from strong unions, who, as a result of their struggle, have been able to obtain cars. That is where we are promoting it, because in the street it would be difficult for us to sell batteries. There would be a blockade on sales.

That's the hope we have, to be able to create our own jobs. I am on a blacklist of all the companies. Forget it. I can't go to a company. I'm not going to get a job, so how am I going to survive? We hope this plan succeeds, because the goals of this project are good. Workers could find themselves in the same situation as us—it wouldn't be unusual for that to happen—that compañeros from other unions are left without a source of income to survive. So we could help by providing jobs, or by creating a strike fund for our compañeros.

This project includes the thirteen fired workers? What are your next steps?

Right now the compañeros are going around trying to get wood to make our small workshop. It's going to be a little workshop, nothing luxurious, just a simple structure. The compañeros are building that now, but we still are lacking things to be able to start working. But with the little that we have, we are going to see what we can do to be able to start to work. Because if we don't take the first step, we can't begin to walk. We have to take the first step, which is to build the shack where we are going to work.

You have exhausted all legal recourses, and there is no way to win the case?

No. The conflict, the labor relations between the company and us, no longer exists. After the first round, which was ruled in our favor, the second round negated our right to reinstatement. Worse than that, they threw us out. The court ordered the case to be canceled. We'd been in this struggle for twenty-nine months, and according to the Labor Code we had to be paid for that time because the company illegally closed the factory. It was an illegal lock-out. Two things, the illegal stoppage and a management substitution, obligated the owner to pay us for all the time we were involved in the process. These same judges, in complicity with the owners, didn't recognize more than eight of the twenty-nine months. So they didn't give us even half of what we were entitled to.

And since the Constitutional Court—the highest legal body of our country—issued its last opinion, saying there would be no reinstatement, we had nowhere to turn. We had to accept that judgment. We were badly off economically. We couldn't reject what they gave us, the eight months' pay. It gave us something, even if only to pay the debts we had accumulated for having spent so much time without working.

I understand that within the labor movement there is concern that the case of Acumuladores Victor is going to be seen as a deterrent to other workers' forming unions. Workers are going to see the experience you had, and they are going to conclude that they cannot struggle because they will end up without jobs for two or three years. How do you see the spirits of people in the labor movement in light of the experience of the workers of Acumuladores Victor?

I personally have spoken about this with other compañeros. Our experience has its positive and negative sides. On the negative side, some compañeros in other unions who are involved in labor conflicts may conclude that they are struggling for nothing: "The Acumuladores Victor workers didn't achieve anything; it's better for us to abandon the struggle before the same thing happens to us." It could be that some workers think this way.

On the positive side, owners may see that what was done to us was costly. They're likely to say, "If we leave these workers locked outside, the same thing will happen to us as happened to Acumuladores Victor." The labor problems lasted for so long, so much money was invested to defeat us, and they had to do it illegally.

So it does have its positive and negative elements. Owners are going to have to think twice before they lock out their workers. They aren't going to do it just to do it, because they aren't going to achieve what they want easily. There is a positive side for the working class because now the owners are going to think first: what hurts them most is their pocketbooks' losing money. And these gentlemen lost money. So others are going to think about it. They will have to analyze its positive and negative aspects. The compañeros should think about this, too; they shouldn't just look at the negative but the positive as well.

Would you still have joined this struggle if you had known that the factory would be illegally closed and you would spend almost three years trying to save your jobs and create a union?

I'm going to tell you something. We knew that this was going to happen. When we were inside the company, and they hadn't yet closed operations, the company's legal adviser told us that they were going to shut down the factory. And about fifteen days after they closed the factory, Don Victor and his legal adviser told us that we would spend two or three years struggling. "Whoever is able should save himself first," they told us.

Yes, we knew what was going to happen to us. We knew that they would carry out their threats against us and the union. But we had to show them our strength, our pride, as unionists. We had to show them that money isn't everything in life.

In the long run, we held up. We gave them a fight. We made them suffer. We knew it wasn't going to be easy, that the struggle was going to last a long time. And Don Victor, the factory owner, left for the United States when he became ill.

Do you regret what you did?

No, I don't regret it. On the contrary, if there were another opportunity to work in another factory and organize another union, I would gladly do it.

*Let's go back to the topic of fear that some compañeros have because of
their involvement in the labor movement. Don't you feel afraid sometimes? As your father says, maybe they will kidnap you, assassinate you.
Do you have those fears, and how do you confront them?*

I am a person who believes in God. I have always said to people
that we all have the right to think what we want. Some compañeros have become so involved in the labor movement that they
have stopped believing in He who created us. But I believe in Him,
and I've never been afraid. Through Him, each one has his hour
and his destiny in life, and our lives are in His hands. I believe in
Him; thanks to God, I have been at peace.

Although they have come looking for me, and although sometimes I arrive at home very late in the night because of my work, I
live my life in peace. It doesn't worry me that something could
happen to me, because if it does, it would be because it was my day.
One creates his own fear.

Please tell us about your music group.

I was born with a musical instinct. When I was in night school,
there were contests for Mother's Day and Father's Day, and I always
won first place in the songs. I sang, but I couldn't play the guitar
because I hadn't had the opportunity to learn. My teacher in primary school played piano, and he accompanied me.

I always liked to sing music that had a protest message. I used to
sing "Casas de Carton," "Yo No Puedo Callar" ["I Can't Keep
Quiet"], and "Ayer Tuve un Sueno" ["Last Night I Had a Dream"].
Those songs are the ones I liked to sing. So I always loved music,
but there was never anyone to organize us. But later a compañero
who played the guitar encouraged us to organize the group.

After he left the group, we needed a guitar player since those of
us who were left played the bongos and sang. None of us knew how
to play the guitar. You know, it's hard to find a compañero to join
the group unless he's involved in the labor movement because of
the type of music we play. Unfortunately, very few compañeros in
the labor movement are able to play guitar.

So that's how I began to want to learn to play guitar. Now I'm
learning, and I know some songs. We found another compañero

who also can play the guitar very well. So we formed a group, and we even recorded a song. At that time the government was talking a lot about raising bus fares, so we composed a song against this idea.

Where do you play? Where do you give performances?

This past Friday we had a gathering here in the UNSITRAGUA offices to commemorate the termination of our conflict. The anniversary of the compañeros of Coca-Cola is coming up, and if they invite us we are going to perform there also. For a while the group went unnoticed, but now we have an invitation to go to Mexico.

A translation of the song "Casas de Carton"

How sad the rain sounds on the cardboard roofs.
How sad my people who live in their houses of cardboard.
The worker comes down.
Almost dragging his steps from the weight of his suffering.
Look how much he has suffered.
Look how much his suffering weighs him down.

Uphill he leaves his wife pregnant.
Below is the city, and he gets lost in its maze.
Today is the same as yesterday.
It's a world without tomorrow.
How sad the rain sounds on the cardboard roofs.
How sad my people live in their houses of cardboard.

Children the color of my land with the same scars.
Millionaires of worms.
And for that reason,
how sad the children who live in the houses of cardboard.

How happily the dogs live in the house of the exploiter.
You aren't going to believe it, but there are schools for dogs.
And they give them education so they won't bite the daily papers.
But as of many years ago, the boss is biting the worker.
How sad the rain sounds on the roofs of cardboard.
How far away hope is from the houses of cardboard.

2

ANGEL

A Commitment That
Involves the Entire Family

Although many labor leaders, lawyers, and teachers were lost during the heavy repression of the late 1970s to the mid-1980s, a handful managed to survive that time and were invaluable in the movement's efforts to re-establish itself, which began about 1985. Angel is one such leader who watched many of his companions fall but who stayed in Guatemala to fight for economic and social rights for workers.

Angel's perspective is particularly valuable because he has lived through what some others in this book have only heard or read about. He also exemplifies the sacrifices some make to continue this work; he describes attacks on his children and a time when he was kidnapped and drugged. Angel has experienced difficulties with his health, as well as constant death threats, because of his participation in the movement for workers' rights. Yet his commitment remains unfailing, and his persistent presence in Guatemala serves as a challenge to the authorities trying to destroy the labor movement.

So far, Angel has won this contest, although the political reality of Guatemala puts the outcome continually in doubt. It was difficult to get Angel to talk about himself in this interview; some things came out only because one of the interviewers, Karen, knows him well. He preferred not to take personal credit for his efforts but rather to share the recognition with others.

This is one of the qualities that makes Angel a respected and recognized leader. He is not someone who constantly appears in the media or in front of the microphone at a rally. He prefers to work quietly behind the scenes, developing other leaders to take his place, and supporting the efforts of younger, less experienced unionists.

When and how did you become involved in the labor movement?

I've spent about fifteen years within the labor movement, although before that I participated in other movements. For example, in the 1970s I worked a lot with marginal groups, organizing the population. Some of this activity was through church groups, such as Christian youth groups. Many Christians were involved in this type of work at that time, and, as we worked with these populations, we identified more with the community.

In some cases, community groups rejected the Catholic movement. It occurred to us to try to get involved with those groups through other kinds of activities, and we did this by working with children. For example, the scout movement was a way that children and youth could be involved and, through them, we could reach adults.[1] The scout movement has some aspects that are a bit out of line with the principles we wanted to carry out. However, we used it as one path to the people, and the experience was very pleasant.

I got to know from the inside the needs of poor people. That made me more empathetic and aware of their problems. Later on I worked as a secondary school teacher and participated in the union as a rank-and-file member. As a member of the teachers' movement at that time, I participated in the 1975 strike, a historic event within the movement. That strike taught us a lot about popular activities.

I left teaching fifteen years ago, and began to work in the private sector. Ever since then, I have been part of the union where I currently work. I became part of the directorate, as the general secretary of the union, only two months after I started working there.

1. The scout movement in Guatemala is similar to the Boy Scouts and Girl Scouts in the United States.

Members of UNSITRAGUA march in the International Workers' Day parade in Guatemala City. Photo Karen Brandow

What led you to become involved in the popular movement?

As I said, there was this previous experience working with the poor. And I had worked in the teachers' efforts. I saw it from an altruistic point of view; I identified with the needs of the population. Getting involved with the labor movement and understanding its significance makes a person more committed. I took it very seriously, which is what that commitment demanded.

My union was in a flowering period when I joined. It had just been organized—now the union is seventeen years old—so it was very young at that time. There was a lot of enthusiasm and participation on everyone's part, including the directorate and the rank and file.

An important element in my union is its high percentage of participation by women—about 85 percent. When I joined, the entire leadership was made up of women. The directorate proposed that men also assume leadership responsibilities. This was a challenge to the men to act with the same degree of responsibility as the compañeras, since the men were lagging behind and the women were assuming responsibility for the union. I admired the women leaders for doing this.

Later, after we had affiliated with another union that was thriving at the time, some of the leaders were assassinated. Other compañeros had to go into exile to save their lives. Those compañeros, like many others, gave a lot to the federation and are still active in the labor movement. They had a contagious charisma, which motivated workers to participate in the union with the same degree of resolve.

Then history-making events took place within the Guatemalan labor movement and popular movement. One of the most important was the creation of the National Committee of Labor Unity (CNUS).[2] That's when I became involved. It was the formative era for the Guatemalan labor movement; the members made high demands on themselves and one another. This obligated us to participate, an obligation I interpret as a commitment to the compañeros, to the movement, and to the people.

2. The CNUS (Comite Nacional de Unidad Sindical), or National Committee of Labor Unity, is one of the historic labor organizations that was formed in the 1970s.

Tell us about your personal life. When did you get married?

I got married in 1975.

At that time, did you discuss the labor movement and your commitment to the movement with your compañera?

There is something important that I must tell you here about my compañera. When she and I were young, we were a part of the Christian movement. We participated together. Later, we also joined the teachers' movement. So there was no difficulty between us with respect to the labor movement. The commitment has not been mine alone; it has been hers as well. And my children are committed; they understand and participate in the movement. It's an expression of how much we identify with and struggle for our class—the working class.

A few years after you began your involvement with the labor movement, there was a period of heavy repression against it and other popular movements. How did that period affect you? Did you or your family or friends have problems with the repression?

The repression has been widespread and has affected all of us in one way or another. Repression involves both physical violence and psychological violence. All unionists, both members of the directorate and rank-and-file members, need to confront the repression of owners and the government, struggle for the right to organize and engage in collective bargaining, and demand a free labor movement.

Violence against the labor movement is a permanent issue, and one lives with repression. Obviously, the repression has worsened and lessened, and at that time the levels were higher. During the late 1970s and early 1980s, we lived through a lot of anguish as a result of it. I remember well having to look for safe houses in which to hold our meetings. Many of my compañeros from that time are no longer with us. They were assassinated, kidnapped, or forced to leave the country. We all had to be concerned about safety measures. We lived through threats and personal harassment. The union lived through this, as did the federation. We had to respond to these threats collectively and create defense mechanisms to protect ourselves. It was an ongoing situation.

My wife's sister was kidnapped on August 24, 1980, along with the compañeros of Emaus.[3] That kidnapping affected us deeply. She had lived with us, and she was my wife's only sister. She was a member of our family, and it hurt us all. The loss presented a challenge to the family about continuing with the union. We decided we had to continue the struggle. I don't think it's a question of valor or spontaneity but rather that the work had to go on. Our commitment, and particularly my commitment, had to continue within the labor movement and in popular movement activities. So that's what we did. We continued to be active, although obviously we had to reflect about the need for personal security. Eventually, that particularly difficult period ended, although difficult times have not passed.

Was your wife's sister a unionist?

Yes, she was.

What other kinds of security problems have you had over the years?

I have been more affected by security problems in recent years. That's not to say that there weren't problems before, because there were. But lately the problems have been more intense. The death threats have been almost constant, with telephone threats to my home, to my office, to the union office. Now that my participation has been more open, such as my work in the UNSITRAGUA office, the repression has affected me.

In 1988 I was intercepted as I went to my house after having visited a picket line involving some compañeras on strike at a factory. When I left the unionists, I was accosted by two men and two women. They detained me in a car, and they beat me. They threatened me with death. And they injected me with some drug that made me lose consciousness for about eleven hours. I appeared on the doorstep of my house, lying there after having been beaten. The physical blows were tolerable, but the drug made me lose my

3. On August 24, 1980, seventeen labor leaders were kidnapped from a labor education center in Escuintla called Emaus. This was the third major kidnapping of labor leaders that year.

memory. It took about a week for me to re-orient myself. Later, this same vehicle appeared in the parking area of the central plaza, a curious thing since only members of the army park there.

Later I was operated on for a tumor that had grown on the right side of my leg. According to the medical diagnosis, the tumor resulted from the blows I'd received in the beating.

My activity with the union was discussed not only within my family but also among the compañeros. We came to the conclusion that I should continue my commitment with the same schedule of activity. This decision to continue was made despite the fact that my wife had been accosted on the road a few days earlier. The men told her that she should tell me to withdraw from my activities or my family and home would be bombed. She had been intercepted at the door of our house about four days before the discussion about my future activities in the labor movement. These threats were denounced at the international level and received widespread publicity.

Another time, the bolts on my wheels were removed, and, when I drove the car, the wheels went one way and the car went the other! That was a few days after I was captured and suffered the beating.

Other problems have occurred. Recently my older son, who is fourteen, was assaulted on five different occasions, supposedly by thieves. Each attack was near our house. In the past two weeks, I suffered another assault. Two men robbed me. Eight days later they assaulted me again, but this time they cut me with a knife. The only things they took were a sweater and an umbrella. And this was at four thirty in the afternoon, practically in the center of downtown Guatemala City! I had just left a union meeting when I was attacked.

Given the large number of assaults on my son and me—seven in all—it's doubtful that these were really just instances of common crime. Rather, they're the everyday circumstances of the current political situation in Guatemala.

How does all of this affect you physically?

It has affected me a great deal. It's not easy to heal from a beating at my age. The recuperation is slow, and emotionally, too, it clearly takes its toll. It has made me reflect about many things, particularly about my family. I wish what happened to my son had happened to me instead.

My wife and I maintain strict security measures for the children. We leave them at the door of the school each day, and, if at all possible, we pick them up after school. It's hard because we have commitments at work and at home, but we try to share as much as possible in their activities. However, this protectiveness doesn't mean we're encouraging them to become introverted. We try not to impose our concerns on them.

The things that have happened to our family have been tough: a kidnapping, the beatings, and the continuing physical effects. The threats to my wife. The assaults on our older son. We need to be aware of the children's security twenty-four hours a day. When they go to school, my wife and I are thinking of the hour they're going to leave and the hour they're going to arrive. When they have an extracurricular activity, we give them instructions about protecting themselves. Sometimes we may go too far. Perhaps we are unconsciously creating overprotected children, but considering what has happened to our family, we don't know what else to do.

How have these events affected your children?

The children certainly have been affected, particularly the oldest. He has suffered assaults, beatings, and intimidation—gross, vile, and vulgar intimidation. And whether we want to believe it or not, this has affected him. My other children, who are thirteen and eleven years old, haven't been affected so directly. I do worry about my thirteen-year-old daughter. Sometimes the violence against women is extreme. The anti-unionists try to offend women's dignity, to demonstrate *machismo*. I hope that this type of thing doesn't happen to her.

Do your children understand the labor movement and why these things are happening in their lives?

Yes, definitely. Clearly there was a time when they couldn't understand it, but now they do. My wife and I feel strongly about explaining everything to them and making them see that they should take on the same commitment when they are old enough to do so.

Ours is a commitment that involves the entire family, a commitment as human beings. If my children see that they can do something on behalf of the struggle, they should do it. While their understanding of the struggle can't be at the same level as an adult's, they do comprehend that our family must participate in the union activities.

You have told us that very few of the leaders who began in the struggle with you fifteen years ago are left. After all that you have lived through and witnessed, what gives you the hope and spirit to continue in the struggle?

It has a lot of elements. In the first place, my commitment to the labor movement is a permanent part of my life, not something that comes and goes. I believe that I should contribute something to it every day with a great deal of love and personal surrender. Out of that premise comes hope. We live for that commitment. And we hope and dream for results.

I'm gratified that results have come despite the brutal repression of the movement. Seeing those gains creates a personal satisfaction, because I have made this my life. Also, there are collective satisfactions, for the labor movement and for the population. A result may be small or huge; either way, there are advances. One has to note them and value them. These advances aren't from the contributions of any single individual but from the efforts of all, from labor unity.

Can you give us some examples of the successes you have seen in the labor movement?

There have been so many. If we go back some years, for example from 1975 to 1980, there was repression but there was also organized struggle. And the results were great. I mentioned in the beginning of the interview the creation of CNUS. That is one of the big achievements, the way in which the labor movement was organized with help from other sectors of the popular movement. Political achievements also were won, along with organizational progress. These advances were huge.

This isn't a personal issue or something that I want to boast about. It's an example of the achievements of the labor movement of that time. Not just the directorate but all of us identified with the movement. There was a great deal of participation. I was never anything more than a directorate member of my union, but I was a rank-and-file member of that larger movement.

I remember the last demonstration that took place in that period of major repression, in October of 1980. The situation was very difficult for the labor movement and the popular movement. Many assassinations and many kidnappings occurred. The October 20th march was organized by rank-and-file members of CNUS. The demonstration was the proudest moment of the movement, the greatest political response to the repression, the greatest organized response.

There was a degree of intimidation felt by all the compañeros, but we just had to take up the challenge. Part of the satisfaction was seeing that despite the repression, we continued to be involved. We continued to speak out.

Since the end of 1984, the labor movement has been in a new phase, one of reconstruction. In 1984 and 1985, because the space for political activity was closed—the oppression and repression escalated—we wondered if it was prudent to participate in union activities. Fear reigned. That's how it was. Terrorism is the main tool used by the oppressors. But in spite of the worsening circumstances and our fears, we concluded that there was no alternative but to keep organizing.

I want to be honest. We didn't launch the reorganization of the labor movement, yet the founding of UNSITRAGUA was an important piece of our political and ideological struggle.

Within the current Guatemalan context, is it possible for the labor movement to grow?

Of course. I think that the labor movement is going to grow.

The current political period in Guatemala, the so-called democratization process, is nothing more than an attempt by the groups in power to create and mobilize their forces, to have a greater degree of control beyond what they have traditionally had, and to maintain power. This process has the potential to destroy the labor movement. Yet five years have passed, and that hasn't happened. The labor movement has found its voice, and the popular movement in general has developed within its limitations.

We can't say that we are in the best of conditions. There are limitations. But at least the Committee of Peasant Unity, the CUC, now acts with a certain degree of legitimacy. Two or three years ago, it had to act as though it were a group of insurgents, but now the situation has improved some. We also have CONAVIGUA, CERJ, and GAM, and all are still active.[4] There really has been an organizational response, and this has been a setback for those attempting to contain the popular movement. Clearly there is greater repression, but the labor movement can grow. Despite the fact that the government has tried to neutralize and destroy it, the movement keeps going.

The public sector workers of FENASTEG are an example of how robust the movement is.[5] They show us that the labor movement has to be intelligent and creative and that it must look for its own alternatives. These characteristics will make the labor movement continue to grow.

With all the problems you have had to confront, did it ever cross your mind to drop out of the struggle?

I don't want to commit the sin of seeming very courageous or anything like that, because as a human being a person has his or her limits. At times I have thought about withdrawing from a particular role or leadership position, but only as a result of the personal differences that occur within the movement. I have never considered withdrawing from the struggle itself.

Is there anything you'd like to say to the people of the United States? Anything you'd like them to know?

Yes. There is something that we all understand: the people of the United States are not synonymous with their government. We iden-

4. The CONAVIGUA (Coordinadora Nacional de Viudas de Guatemala), or National Coordination of Guatemalan Widows, currently has thirteen thousand members who struggle against human rights violations in the countryside and for governmental compensation for the women and children who have lost their male family members to violence. The CERJ (Consejo Etnico Runejel Junam), or Council of Ethnic Communities Runejel Junam, organizes rural communities to resist forced participation in the constitutionally voluntary Civil Defense Patrol.

5. The FENASTEG (Federación Nacional de Sindicatos de Trabajadores del Estado de Guatemala) is the National Federation of Unions of State Workers. Public-sector workers were not allowed to unionize from 1954 until 1986.

tify with the people, and we are brothers and sisters. Those who lead the destiny of the North American people have responsibility in given circumstances or particular moments, but they are not the people. We have obtained much solidarity from the North American people, and from many other people, because they have understood not only our situation but also the situation of other repressed peoples. Many North Americans have committed themselves generously, in some cases beyond what they can reasonably give. Perhaps this is a lot to ask, but we expect that of the North American people.

We also believe that they should question the attitudes and policies of the United States government that go against the Latin American people. They should become part of a questioning process and denounce injustices.

What Latin American people long for most is peace and national reconciliation. These goals entail human rights, social justice, and an authentic democracy. To achieve these, we need the support of the North American people. Peace really means that there is no more infant mortality, hunger, or discrimination in all senses of the word. That would be my message for the North American people, and a commitment that we share.

Let's go back to the discussion about the tremendous amount of pressure and uncertainty you live with because of your participation in the labor movement. You don't know from one day to the next what is going to happen to your family. Why do some people react to this situation by fleeing the country, while others like yourself stay and persist in the struggle?

There are many different ways to react to our situation. The compañeros who leave must be understood. The pressures here are great, and the repression is so extreme that some can't live with those pressures. So the alternative is self-preservation.

There have been many martyrs. But there are also lives that have been spared, compañeros who continue to work independently wherever they are. If they have identified with the struggle, with the work, they are going to continue to contribute no matter where they are or at what level they are. We have that expectation of compañeros. If they leave, it is because of the pressures.

People have different emotional states. One could question the motives of those who leave, but in a nonjudgmental way. Some compañeros may take advantage of circumstances, and look for justifications to leave. But if compañeros are honest and say, "I don't want to struggle anymore, I have my limitations," that's fine. We can't judge them, because we may also fall into that kind of situation.

There are those who stay but who distance themselves from union activities. They don't end up in a more comfortable position. They can't be comfortable having said, "I'm leaving, I'm dropping out, I'm going to devote myself to other activities. I'm going to ignore what is happening. I'm going to ignore the movement." If I were to drop out and say, "I'm going to live better. I'm going to eat better. My children are going to be better dressed, and they aren't going to have pressures," I would be deceiving myself. Hardships are always going to surround me, and maybe conditions will worsen.

Those of us who remain active, those of us who remain committed, do so even though we are conscious that our families are affected. This isn't an irresponsible attitude; it's an effort to look at the difficulties as a personal sacrifice for the greater good. In a given moment, the circumstances might not allow me to continue to be so involved, and the alternative would be to leave. I don't know. I don't want to think about it, but the repression might force me to leave someday. As I said, as long as one can view those circumstances in a broad perspective, and seek alternatives to repression, one can say to oneself, "I'm staying, and I'll continue to work."

Not just in my case, of course; many compañeros do it. We all have problems, and we consult with each other. We try to share solutions so that we can continue the struggle. When one looks to his or her compañeros and finds unconditional support and friendship, there's a wonderful feeling of solidarity. We give each other that kind of support. There is friendship. That is one of the alternatives.

Sometimes it seems that it's a game of Russian roulette. One continues, hoping that tomorrow or the next day they won't get you and you'll have the chance to choose another path if that's necessary. But a person never knows if he or she is going to have that chance.

Yes, it is like Russian roulette. But perhaps within that Russian roulette there is a moment with alternatives. That is what we hope.

3

CLARA

The Terrible Anguish

The memories of recent repression remain fresh in the minds of all Guatemalans. Thus, it is no longer "necessary" for the government to carry out such extreme actions to engender high levels of fear in unionists and their families. An occasional kidnapping or assassination gets the message across quite clearly: this could happen to you, too, if you continue to participate in union activities. Moreover, the policy of repression has changed to one in which rank-and-file participants and family members are as vulnerable as union leaders to acts of repression. This is in part so as not to arouse a great deal of international reaction by harming a nationally known leader of the labor movement.

For those who carry out violent actions, it appears to be a matter of routine. The psychological and economic consequences for the affected families, however, are intense and lifelong. This is illustrated in the testimonies of three women interviewed, whose husbands were victims of anti-union repression.

Although each woman has dealt with her suffering in her own way, some of the common themes include a sense of depression and helplessness, emotional and scholastic problems for their children, severe economic difficulties, and a frustrated desire for justice.

The fact that two of the women did not wish themselves to be publicly identified illustrates the level of fear they experience, which in Guatemala's current political climate is justified. They feel even more vulnerable because they are the sole source of economic and moral support for their children. None of the three has entered into another life partnership, perhaps because they cannot let go of their memories of an assassinated or disappeared compañero, and perhaps because the wife of an assassinated or disappeared unionist is too risky a compañera for most Guatemalan men.

The most inspiring aspect is that despite all they have suffered, each of these women remains active in the movement, via interviews with the international press, speaking tours, and affiliation with a union. Their stories are three among thousands of similar ones in Guatemala, which could be told by all the compañeras of victims of repression and violence. We are deeply appreciative that they were willing to share these painful experiences with us, in what were for us the most emotionally difficult interviews to carry out. Clara's interview appears below, and the other two appear in Chapters 8 and 9.

Clara is the wife of one of the twenty-seven union leaders kidnapped from the offices of the CNT on June 21, 1980, the largest mass disappearance in Guatemalan history.[1] It was the second mass kidnapping of labor leaders that year (the first took place after the May Day march), and it left the movement destroyed. Like most other cases of disappearances, the case was never investigated—even though it is publicly known that the National Police were responsible—and none of the twenty-seven was ever heard from again.

Clara discusses how this event has affected her and her family since 1980.

When you first met your husband, was he already involved in the labor movement?

No, not yet. My husband decided to join the union later on because there was so much injustice, so much mistreatment, in the places he worked. He saw that the compañeros who weren't orga-

---

1. The CNT (Central Nacional de Trabajadores) is the National Workers' Central.

Don Oscar holds a picture of his disappeared daughter. The caption under her picture reads "We weep [from] your absence. May 3." He vowed never to shave until she appeared again. Photo Joe Gorin

nized were mistreated. The managers made them work more than the normal amount. If the managers wanted to pay them for a holiday, they did; if not, the workers weren't paid.

On the other hand, my husband looked at those who were organized. He saw that they placed demands on their companies. Yes, it took a lot of struggle to get management to comply with their demands, a lot of struggle, but these workers were better off than those who weren't organized.

When my husband worked in one factory, the compañeros said to him, "Join us! If you don't, the managers are going to fire you." He said, "No, perhaps they won't fire me." But one day they did fire him, and the compañeros said, "Now you see! If you had joined the union when we told you to, they couldn't have fired you!" My husband spent some time without a job. Then he worked in another job, and from there he went to another factory, where there was a union.

What year was that?

That was in 1974 or 1975.

And he joined the union?

Yes. After a few months he realized the compañeros had been right. And then the compañeros began to teach him about unions.

How did you feel when your husband joined the union?

Well, at that time there hadn't been so much repression—in those years unionists wouldn't be disappeared. Yes, the unionists were punished. They were detained. They were removed from some workplaces. For example, the CNT had been broken into two times, but the government only sent the unionists to detention headquarters. There they beat the unionists and tortured them. The government did this so that people would stop their union activities. But the government always let the unionists go free eventually.

I knew that in time it would be my husband's turn to be taken away. A while before, he told me that they had captured a compañero. They held this compañero in the first or second police headquarters, where they beat him. Now my husband had to be careful. He had to be in hiding.

So you spoke about the risks of being in the labor movement, and you talked about the possibility of something happening to him one day?

Not at first. In the beginning I wasn't afraid. I wasn't worried. I became more worried as time went on.

When they began to see that he was more involved in the union, they came to look for him. There was a plant manager, a friend of his, who told him, "Look, don't get involved with those unionists. You're very well behaved, and things will go badly for you here if you're involved with the union. I'll look for another position for you where you can earn more money."

My husband told me all that. Then he said to me, "I'm already unionized. I'm a member. I want to help the compañeros because management commits injustices in the workplace. Recently they kicked a compañero. If you get involved and speak up to defend him, the same thing befalls you. But if you're affiliated with the union, you can defend yourself!"

So you supported his participation in the union, or were you afraid that something would happen to him?

At the beginning, yes, I supported his activities. I even felt happy about it. Then when I began to hear that they had killed a student, or that a peasant had appeared dead, that a unionist . . . It made me so sad, and when he began to tell me about these things, I became concerned.

Then they began to look for him again. They came to the house when they knew he wasn't there. They knew that my husband wasn't home, and I told them, "He isn't here, he's at work." They said, "Tell him that we are waiting for him in the Trebol, that we have a good job for him at the Trebol.[2] We'll wait for him at eight o'clock."

When he came home I gave him the message, and he said that I shouldn't pay attention to them. He told me of a man whom the

---

2. The Trebol is a cloverleaf intersection in Guatemala City where several major roads come together.

boss had put there among the unionists—an informant, a traitor. "He is one of those from the company who is trying to terrorize everyone so that we stop this struggle," he told me. "But you shouldn't pay attention." I wasn't afraid then.

A short time afterward, the men came again asking for him. They said they would wait for him in the Trebol. "What kind of arrangement do you have with someone," I asked my husband, "that they wait for you in the Trebol?" "I don't have arrangements with anybody," he said. "It's the bosses who are sending these people to scare us, to see if we'll stop the struggle. But that won't happen. This gives us more strength!" And I began to feel afraid that something would happen to my husband.

Then Lucas García came into power and began to commit barbarities.[3] I've told you that the CNT had been broken into several times, but people had never been disappeared before. Yet since that time, since García, families have been left with a great deal of fear. We were afraid even to go look for them once they had disappeared, because the police scolded us whenever we went to detention centers or the morgue. It was incredible! We had searched as a group. We weren't doing anything wrong. We were just their relatives—wives, mothers, brothers, and sisters.

That day, June 21, 1980, how did you find out what had happened to the unionists?

Well, in the first place, my husband didn't come home that afternoon. It was a Saturday, and all our relatives were waiting for him at my mother's house. He had told me, "Go to your mother's. I'm coming home early. I'll be there around five o'clock. The meeting will be about two hours long."

But he didn't come to my mother's house. Five o'clock passed, and he didn't come. "Perhaps there was some delay," I thought. At that moment I didn't foresee what was happening.

However, on the six o'clock news they said that the CNT had been broken into by government security forces. I felt alright even then, because if the security forces had detained them, then the next day,

---

3. Lucas García was president of Guatemala from 1978 to 1982.

or on Monday, when the relatives arrived at the detention center, the unionists would be let go.

That was not the case. We went on Monday to the CNT office, all the relatives, and we saw a scene of terror there. Everything was chaotic. Chairs had been thrown around, as if used in self-defense. Who knew what had happened? There were pools of blood and signs of the unionists having been dragged to the ground floor.

At that moment, all the relatives were in a horrible, nervous state. We began to look for them, to try to find out where they were being detained. We went to the detention headquarters, and the officials said the unionists were not there. They made fun of us, and when we went around the corner they laughed at us. We said to each other, "They must be there, that's why they're laughing! They are saying they're not there, but they must have them here!"

And so we returned to the CNT office. A woman with very young children, who had just had a baby, was with us. Some of our group had told her not to go to the detention center because, since she was breast-feeding, her baby might be harmed. But she said, "How am I going to find out! I don't have anyone who can go to find out what happened to them!" In those days, I left my son in the care of my mother. At times I didn't even remember that I had a small son and what condition he was in.

How old was your son?

He was four years old. It was hard for him to walk. Although he was four years old, he didn't walk well yet. He needed a lot of help and attention. And I forgot about him! I arrived home in the afternoon and said, "Oh, I left my son with my mother!" But that was how I was—all out of control!

How many relatives of the disappeared were there?

About twenty, when all the relatives came. Later on fewer came, because of the fear that something would happen to us.

We were threatened. The secretary of the CNT received anonymous threats—phone calls, telegrams, letters. They'd say, "Stop looking for your relatives. If you make a scandal, you all will be kidnapped!" Who would not be afraid at that time? So with that fear we no longer went as a group to try to find them; each one looked on her own. It was always worse that way, because to go and say that your husband disappeared in such and such a place always resulted in one's being watched.

Soon after, we were at the CNT office again for a meeting. Someone knocked on the door as if they were going to knock it down. We all were afraid. Some went to hide. I stayed with the CNT secretary because, at that moment, she was getting a call from the Supreme Court saying that my husband and the compañera Irma Candelaria Pérez were being charged in court.

The secretary said, "Let's all go to the court! They must all be there!" But the telephone call was a lie. We arrived at the courthouse and were told, "We haven't made any call from here. They aren't here, and we don't know anything about any unionists. We don't know anything here." We came back feeling very sad. One woman, the mother of one of the disappeared, fainted because she hadn't eaten breakfast. She no longer had any appetite, thinking about her son, concerned about what had happened to him, and if the unionists were going to reappear.

In that way two days went by, then a week, and they still hadn't appeared. We hoped that they were being held someplace, and commissions were formed to look into the detention centers in the various departments. Mr. Villagrán Kramer, the vice president of Guatemala, told some of the compañeros that the unionists were in Berlin, that we should go look for them there.[4] He told the compañeros that we would find them there.

Berlin is a military unit. We formed a commission to try to find them at Berlin. I wanted to go with the commission, but a compañera said to me, "It's better if you don't go. Others of us are going, but you shouldn't go. Remember your son." So I couldn't go because of my son.

This compañera, who works in the Coca-Cola factory, has been very good to me since we met at the time of the disappearances. She has always supported me and helped me decide what we should or shouldn't do. She also had a small daughter at the time, but she had someone there to take care of her child.

---

4. Francisco Villagrán Kramer was vice president during the Lucas García government. He resigned before the end of his term in protest of the atrocities committed by the García regime.

We arranged for a group of four people to go into Berlin. The plan had been that two would stay outside and two would enter the military unit, and if those two were stuck inside, the two outside would report it. But when they arrived at the military unit, only one stayed outside and three went in.

The three were allowed in but only where it was easy to see. The three later said that there were secret jails there, but they were not permitted to see everything, just two or three places, and the officials opened the doors. "Look and see if these are the ones you are searching for," the officials told them. "If it isn't them, you don't get to look anywhere else."

And there were prisoners, people jailed there?

Yes, there were prisoners in there.

Do you have any idea who is responsible for the disappearances?

Yes, it was the Lucas García government, because he was in power at the time.

Why would the government do such a thing?

Since Lucas García was on the side of the rich, the powerful, he thought that by disappearing unionists he would make unions disappear. That is what they wanted. They have always wanted to destroy unions. They have constantly pursued that end. Today we still have compañeros who are threatened and who have to flee, to leave Guatemala.

So the women went to the military unit?

Yes, and they came back without any news, in spite of the fact that Vice President Francisco Villagrán Kramer had assured them that their relatives could be found there. Villagrán Kramer had told them to go to Berlin, that he was certain that they were there. But it was untrue; they were not there.

I don't remember all the details now, but commissions were formed to go to various departments in search of the disappeared. I tell you that because of the increasing fear of the relatives: We thought if this happened to the unionists, then the same could happen to us. We only went to hospitals after that, not to military units. When we heard that such and such number of cadavers appeared in such and such a place—because at that time that was the style, bodies were appearing all over the place—we went and always discovered that it wasn't our relatives. Cadavers appeared in Amatitlán, near the Pacaya volcano, in many different places.

There was an accident in Jutiapa, at a place called the Vuelta de Sonora. Reports said that twenty-seven bodies had appeared, and we said, "It's our relatives!" But since I didn't have money to go that far, I couldn't join the group that went to search for the compañeros. But the group returned and said, "No, it wasn't them, not even one of them."

Other commissions were formed to look for the disappeared. I gave a picture of my husband to my friend. But they came back with the same news. The compañeros had found out that there were graves, but not those of our relatives.

After about three months, I would tell people, "My husband is disappeared," and they would say to me, "Don't look for him." Then in Escuintla some bodies appeared in the grass. "Don't look for them there," people told me. "They say the bodies were thrown in the ocean. They say they were thrown into the Motagua River."

How did you feel when people told you to stop looking for them?

Extremely sad. I fainted when a woman said that to me. When I returned home my mother saw my face, and she said to me, "You are so pale! What happened to you?" I had cried the whole way home. I could find no consolation. A compañera was with me. "Get hold of yourself," she said, "What can we do, if it turned out that way?" But I wasn't consoled.

How old were you at that time?

At that time I was thirty-four years old.

And my mother said to me, "I think you should stop looking for your husband, because you are doing harm to yourself. Resign yourself to it. I am sure they killed him, but what can you do? The only thing we can do is to pray for them, because that is what's best. If they are alive, our prayers will reach them; and if they are dead, the same." My mother said, "Let's not find out any more," because she saw what was happening to me.

We heard many rumors in those days. When we spoke with compañeros who had been imprisoned, they told us, "In such and such a place there are secret jails." And when they began to tell me details about the secret jails, I became sick. "In such and such a place they had prisoners in a tunnel." They told me the case of a woman who had lost her husband. They had kidnapped her husband, and this woman went looking all over for him. They said that when she arrived at a military installation, they let her in. They opened the door to a tunnel and let her walk through the whole tunnel. They gave her a flashlight so she could look at the faces of all who were chained there. They were no longer alive but cadavers and skeletons.

This woman didn't find her husband. When she finished looking at all the prisoners, it is said that she was told, "If you say one word about this to anyone, we will kill you." So she left there terrorized. Her compañeros told her, "You must leave Guatemala. If not, they'll kill you." She had to flee the country.

I believe that military base was in Quiché.[5] But because of all the things I have been through, all the problems I have been through, so many things I have been told, I have forgotten some of the details. I would like to have a memory like a tape recorder. It's impossible with so much suffering. How horrible to think that one of the men this woman saw could have been my husband! That is how we were, going from one place to another—to hospitals, to the morgue, seeing those mutilated bodies.

During one of those commission visits, I thought I saw my husband. My mother said I was mistaken, but I saw that it was my husband there. "Mama, here he is," I told her. But she said to me, "That's not him. His hair wasn't so curly. Look, this body has curlier hair. Control yourself!"

"It's him! it's him!" I told her. "No," she said, "it isn't him. Let's go outside." But I saw that it was him. "Look," she said, "is that his

5. Quiché is a province in the Guatemalan highlands, one of the areas hardest hit by past and current repression.

clothing?" "But they might have changed the clothes," I said. "Look, the boots, the clothing, the hair, everything is the same!" "No, it's not him. His hair wasn't so curly. Look, this body has curlier hair; control yourself!" I stayed with that idea that it could have been him. But my mama told me, "No, it's not him."

We had to walk around with cotton and alcohol; it was nearly impossible to be there because of the smell. It wasn't just one time, but several times. It was making us sick, smelling the stench of dead bodies. We suffered.

It affected my children a lot. At that time my daughter got this idea that her father wasn't dead, even though the newspapers and television said he was dead. So people came and said to me, "Wasn't your husband in the union? Wasn't he disappeared?" "No," I said, "he wasn't in the union." "Then what happened to your husband, why haven't I seen him?" "He went away to work," I told them. "But a group of the CNT was kidnapped, and since you have been so depressed could it be that they kidnapped your husband?" "No," I said. "He left. He went far away, and I get sad." I said this because here it is a crime to be a unionist, and people look upon it with fear. They stay away from you. They stop talking to you, because you're a relative of a unionist.

They asked my daughter, "And your father, where is he?" She was little. "He isn't here," she said, "he went away to work." "No, your father hasn't gone away to work," her little friends told her. "They say your father was killed." This caused a great trauma to my daughter, because she loved her papa so much, and he loved her, too. Even though she was small, she always knew what time he would come home from work and she would go outside to wait for him. "Here he comes, my Papito! Here he comes!" And she'd make a lot of noise as she went out to greet her papa. And she would tell her brother, "Here comes my Papito!"

When he was disappeared, my daughter changed a lot. Before, in her studies, she was happy. Everything stayed with her in kindergarten. But after that, she made herself believe that her papa was far away. I had to take her out of school one day because her little friends said to her, "Your papa is dead." "No," she said, "my papa is not dead! He went far away to work!" "No," said the children, "your papa is dead, because in the news it said that they killed him!"

My daughter came to ask me if this were true, and I told her no, it wasn't true. But her school grades got worse and worse. The teacher had to send for me to see what was happening with the child. I had to move her to a different school, but then she said she didn't want to study anymore.

I didn't want to tell her that her father was killed, but when she was about nine years old she realized it. I had secret meetings with the other women whose husbands had been disappeared. We met clandestinely to continue struggling to find them. June of 1990 was the 10th anniversary of the disappearances. And we never learned anything—where they were taken, whether they were killed or if they were still alive. My daughter realized this because I was friends with so many of the women whose husbands were missing.

So you had to explain to your daughter what had happened to her father?

Yes, so then she got very sad. "Why did you tell me my papa was far away?" "So you wouldn't be sad," I told her, "since you loved each other so much." "But now I am very sad," she told me, "because I miss my papa even more!" And she began to lose control of herself. She suffered a nervous attack. She couldn't hold a glass— she dropped it. Her body was shaking so much that I had to get some medicine for her.

Aside from the emotional suffering, I suffered financially because I couldn't work at the time. I didn't have anyone to stay with my son. I held him in my arms and went knocking on doors. I went with only enough money for the bus fare. I told myself that if I found work, then I'd go back home. I'd have enough money for both fares. But it didn't turn out that way because, with a child along, nobody would give me work. I would come back in the same condition, without food for the children.

I couldn't stay where my mother lives because some of our relatives, even though they are family, told me that they didn't want the kind of problems they thought I'd bring. "Look," my uncle told me, "I'm going to tell you something. I never said this to you before. Sometimes you come here to visit your mother, and it's fine that you come to see her. But you can't come here to live with her, no, because I don't want problems because of the union. I'll have nothing to do with those things." My uncle's wife had told him lies, told him that compañeros from the union came looking for me constantly, but that wasn't so.

Have you received other support from the labor movement?

Yes, particularly the Coca-Cola union. In my desperation I said, "What can I do to support these children?" It was such a horrible situation. I didn't have anything to give them to eat because the house where my mother lived belonged to my uncle. "Go home," he told me.

My mother had a small business, a tortilla business, so I was able to work there. I took my son there. I'd help my mother in the business, and she'd give us food. That's how we managed. But when my uncle told me that I had to go home, I lost that support. That made the children suffer a lot. I feel that my children are suffering because they weren't well fed. Now it's affecting them a great deal.

How is it affecting the children?

My daughter feels weak. She doesn't accomplish much in her studies, and last year she told me that she didn't want to study anymore. "Do you know how I feel?" she asked. "Like my head is empty. They are explaining things to me, they are talking to me, but nothing is entering my mind. I don't even know what they are saying to me. Why am I wasting my time in school? I would be better off working. I don't feel good." But Rodolfo Robles has advised me that I should arrange for her to keep studying.[6]

Back when I couldn't feed the children, I decided that I was going to write a letter and seek help from the union. I went to the Coca-Cola union because it is a strong union. And the members heard my requests. I didn't want them to think badly of me. My husband hadn't worked for the Coca-Cola company, yet the unionists knew what that era was like. They realized the situation at that time, and all that I had suffered, the calamities with my children.

What fear I had! What shame! What other doors had I not knocked on asking for help! People would say to me, "Go to such

6. Rodolfo Robles, of the International Union of Foodworkers (UITA).

and such a place and explain," but I couldn't explain because I wanted people to guess what was happening to me—I didn't want to ask for help. As soon as I knocked and they invited me in, I would simply begin to cry. "But what is wrong?" Only one woman could help me. She gave us small amounts of financial support.

Another woman told to me go to a particular place, but the person I was to see, a nun, wasn't there. They told me that she was somewhere else. When I went to the other place, they said she wasn't usually there, that I should go to still another place. There I was, carrying my son all over because he couldn't walk yet, and he was hungry.

I spent a week going back and forth to those places, until one person finally asked me why I wanted to talk to the nun. I said, "To see if she can help find me a job." "Okay," this person said, "but we don't have any economic aid now." "No," I said, "I want to see if she can help me find work, even for half-days." This person asked me if I knew the nun. "Yes," I said, but I really didn't know her.

When the nun came out she said, "You said that you know me, but I don't know you." "Yes, forgive me," I said. Then I began to explain why my situation had made me lie. "But everything I've come to tell you now is not a lie; it's the truth. Forgive me. Because this is a house of assistance, perhaps you can do me the great favor of finding me work. My children haven't eaten."

The Sister paid a lot of attention to me. She asked me where I lived and told me that she would come to my house. "But if what you've told me is a lie," she told me, "I'm not going to give you anything." The next day the Sister came to my house, and she realized that everything I had told her was the truth.

And with that my spirits began to rise. I had thought I was going to allow myself to just die. I didn't concern myself with my appearance. In time I met Rodolfo Robles. I told him what happened to my husband. And he has helped me to get work.

And that's how you've been able to survive? Do you still live apart from your family?

Now, since my mother is no longer living with my uncle, I am with her. I lived with my father-in-law for a while, but there was no support from him. He looked at the children and me with indifference. He only cared about his other grandchildren, the children of his daughters. Those children didn't have a father, not because they were disappeared like my husband, but because these children's fathers had abandoned them. My father-in-law said, "These poor children, I'm not going to let them die of hunger."

But my children, he hasn't given my children anything. Once when I came home late from work, I found my brother-in-law drunk. He was beating on the door, scaring my kids, and the light was out. I was totally soaked from a severe rainstorm, and I had to climb up a steep hill. I arrived home soaked and exhausted, at night, concerned about my children. When I saw the light turned off, I wondered what could be happening. My brother-in-law was there, crazy. I became very angry. I said, "Get out of here before I do something to you! I'll throw something at you! You have no right to be scaring my children!"

The next day I told my father-in-law, "What kind of support am I getting from you. Far from keeping an eye on the children, you allow them to be frightened! You don't do anything for the children. You don't even ask the children, 'Hasn't your Mama come home yet? No? Then eat something until she comes.'" The children said to me, "Mama, we can't stand the hunger anymore. We can't stand it anymore." I had left them *atol* to drink while they waited for me to come.[7] It was such a terrible situation. At times I can't believe I'm here telling the story. I felt as though I would not be able to get out of the situation, that I would not be able to survive. But thanks to some good people, I'm still here.

How has your son been affected?

The truth is that this year, I couldn't take him with me on the bus anymore. I couldn't sustain his studies. When he was younger, I didn't have to pay his bus fare. Before, I'd put him on my lap if we managed to find a seat, and if not I'd carry him in my arms. But now, I have to pay his fare. I hope to get him into a certain institute. They are considering him now. There is a professional who knows my problem; I have received a lot of moral support from her,

---

7. *Atol* is a traditional Guatemalan drink that is usually made of corn or wheat, sugar, and sometimes milk.

and she spoke to the institute on my behalf. She asked that they charge a special price because of my situation, since I didn't have enough to eat, even for a piece of bread, much less being able to buy school supplies or pay bus fares.

I practically wasted away. At night I didn't sleep, thinking about what I could do. I even thought about giving my children away. But I thought, "What am I doing, thinking about giving my children away?" Why? Not to be rid of them. I would give my children away so they wouldn't have to go hungry. So I would know that they would be treated like children. But then I thought, "No, my God, I would be left alone. What would I live for if I were alone. No, I can't give my children away. I have to push ahead. I have to see them grow up." I didn't want to give them up. It just hurt me that they were suffering and going hungry. I was upset.

When we went to the center of town, my son would say to me, "Mama, I smell chicken," and he pulled me to go into Pollo Campero.[8] "My God, I don't even have the bus fare; what can I give this child?" "Let's go in," he said. "No, child, there is no money." He didn't understand what it meant to have or not to have money. "Let's go in!" "Ay, no, my son, I don't have the money." Inside me I was dying.

How have you had the strength to continue to confront all of this?

The truth is that I ask myself that same question. "How is it that I am still here to tell the story?" When I didn't have even a piece of bread to give my children, I used to kneel down and pray to God. Then, my faith was shaken. One night, I heard tremendous footsteps coming. I was about to go to sleep, and I heard enormous footsteps, as though it were a giant man. Huge boots! Boom! boom! boom! until they came to the door. I dropped my Bible and stayed frozen, and I was certain he was going to open the door. Who knows who it was? Oh, my God! I lay down very cold, trembling. After this great scare, I never prayed again. I tell my compañeras about my experiences, and they say that during a crisis is when I should continue to pray most. But not all of us are strong. I feel, in the sense of faith, very weak.

8. Pollo Campero is a restaurant chain that sells cooked chicken.

One time a *licenciada* whom my son studies with told me she would give me work in her house three times a week.[9] It was far away, but we were in such great need that I took the job. After a while, this woman said to me, "I feel you are like family. I'm not afraid to leave you alone in my house. I'm not worried that something will be missing."

I was very conscientious about closing everything carefully so that no one could enter after I left. I spent the whole day there one Saturday, and there was a party next door. The children were playing, singing, eating ice cream. I began to think, "I don't believe that God exists, because while those children are happy, my children are suffering. Trapped. They haven't even had lunch, because I only left them atol. They drink atol every once in a while, until I come home. Atol and the leftover food the licenciada told me I could take home. "Don't leave any leftovers. Take the food. There are beans and cheese."

I began to cry. "Oh, my God," I said, "while my children are trapped, these children have everything. They have a roof over their heads. They have their parents. They have everything they need." And I started to cry again.

A short time afterwards, an acquaintance called me to help take care of a child. She said, "I'm going to give you a few days' work, but don't let go of your other job, because it's just for a short time." And she asked about my daughter and son, about whether the children were going through hard times. She gave me 50 quetzales.[10] "Take this, and buy them some food," she said.

But a few days later while I was ironing, I began to cry. I felt so alone. I thought, "If God exists, why do children suffer?" "He doesn't exist," I thought, "because in the Bible, Jesus says 'Let the children come to me, because children are of the kingdom of heaven.' But this is not so, because my children are suffering, while others are not suffering. Why?"

I asked you where you get the strength to continue. If it isn't through prayer, where does it come from?

9. *Licenciada* is a term used for those who have completed a certain degree of schooling, such as lawyers, accountants, or other professionals.
10. At the time of this interview, 50 quetzales equaled approximately $8.75.

I think from the concern I have for my children. Now I am at the point where my mother helps me by taking care of my son. I feel more relaxed, because now I can go out to work. He can bear not seeing me all day, but at night he always waits for me. He doesn't eat dinner until I come home. They say, "He hasn't eaten because he was waiting for you." And I say, "My son, you must eat, because one day I might die, or I might have to work far away, and you'll be waiting for me to come home!" I explain it to him, though he doesn't understand much. I tell him, "Look, before there was no food. Now there are beans, and there is bread to eat. You have to eat it. When you were smaller, I couldn't give you what you are eating now, even if it's just beans. And now beans are so expensive." He loves beans. "If there is nothing else to eat, son, eat beans. You must eat. Don't wait for me, because if you eat very late you will get sick." But he doesn't understand. He always waits for me. What he wants is to see me and to be with me.

Could you explain the difference between the experience of women whose compañeros have been disappeared, and widows in Guatemala?

I think there is a difference. A widow sees that her husband has died. It hurts that he has died. For widows, at least they know this is true. At least there was a burial. The widow knows where the body is. And in time the children realize that their father has died, that he was buried.

On the other hand, when it's a disappeared relative, I believe it is even more difficult. The years pass. For relatives of the disappeared, it hurts so much because their husbands weren't involved in illegal activities for which they could be killed, but always for just causes. Yes, it hurts very much.

I don't know how it is with all the relatives, but in my case it is very hard to talk about my situation. At times, I can handle it a little, but at other times, no. I become depressed. I start to cry and cry, as though this had happened yesterday. As though it had just taken place, and it's been ten years!

I don't know if all relatives think this way or just us, the spouses. The mothers must feel it even more. It would hurt me so much to see that happen to one of my children. It would kill me.

One has to live with the anguish of what has become of the disappeared. Could they still be alive? What conditions are they in? In what situation? If they were killed, where? Where were they left? How? What did they suffer in that moment?

To this date, I suffer, because when I dream about him I dream that he comes and looks for us. I don't dream of his being dead. I've never dreamt of him as dead. I only dream of him alive. That he came to the house, the first days, in that terrible anguish. In my dreams I feel as though he were going to knock on the door at any moment.

One day, at midnight, someone knocked on the door. I said, "Could that be my husband?" "Who else would be knocking at midnight? It must be my husband!" I got up and opened the window and looked at the door, where my father-in-law was standing.

While I was at my mother's for a few days, a lot of telegrams and letters arrived. I was the first to run and receive them. "Could that be from my husband?" But the telegrams and letters weren't from my husband. When there were knocks on doors, I'd quickly get up. "It must be him!"

But nothing, except a terrible anguish, which I don't think ever leaves you. To this day I hear knocks and I dream of him. I think, "Could it be that they had him far away, and now they have let him go free. And here he comes!" The first days I said, "Perhaps they have escaped! Couldn't it be him? Did he escape?" So many things come to one's mind!

To this day I have been left with the feeling that he could come back at any moment. On the other hand, when a relative is known to be dead, one leaves it to God. Be it a death by violence or by other causes, one says, "I see that he or she is dead, and I must resign myself to it."

But not in this case. For example, my daughter is upset by my answer when people ask me about my husband. She says, "Mama, it hurts me when you say that he is disappeared. Why don't you say what you used to say, that he is working far away?" "People don't believe you when you say that," I tell her. "Even if they don't believe it," she says, "it hurts me when you say he is disappeared, or that he died."

To some people, I say he is dead. But my daughter insists, "Don't say that, Mama! Don't say that my papa is dead!" So the psychiatrist tries to make her face her denial. "You have to accept the reality," she tells her. "You shouldn't be living on illusions, making yourself believe that your father is far away, working." Yet my daughter tells that to her friends. "And your papa? Where is he?" "My papa is far away," she tells them.

But people realize the truth, because if he were really working, our situation would be different. So I tell her, "We wouldn't be living as we are. We would be better off because your papa would send us money. We wouldn't be going through these hardships."

We're not going through as much hardship now as we were before, when sometimes we didn't even eat once a day. If we ate once a day, that was good. Now even though everything is limited, at least we eat three meals daily. At times, I can leave the children with their grandmother while I work. And I don't have to worry that they are alone, that someone is going to enter the house and do them harm. My mother has supported me a great deal, and since my sisters also work they help me with food.

What was the goal of the Group of Women of June 21? And when was the group formed?

It was formed three years after the kidnappings. The goal was to continue searching for the missing. At the least, we wanted information. If they killed them, they should say so. But the government didn't respond to us.

And how did you make these demands? Was it to the government and the judicial system?

That was the idea. The truth is, however, that fear remained in many families. Although they haven't really wanted to, they thought it wiser to keep quiet and not continue the struggle. For example the mother of Irma Candelaria Pérez says, "If my daughter is alive, God be with her and help her. And if she is dead, the same. But I won't struggle anymore, because while my husband was thinking about her, working on a second floor, he fell from there and died." She also has been ill, and she says, "I no longer want to continue in the struggle."[11]

11. Irma Candelaria Pérez is one of the disappeared unionists.

More than anything, it's that attitude. Many people don't want to hear anything more. It isn't that they don't want to know, but that they must make themselves known to the governmental authorities if they struggle, as GAM members do. We no longer feel capable because, you see, at that time we were left very frightened. I told you about the time when they went to knock on the doors of the CNT. All of us were so scared. They say one woman could no longer breast-feed her baby because she became so upset. We thought that they were going to attack us as well and make us disappear. And many people said to me, "Don't go anymore. If your husbands are detained, they will be let go." "Don't keep struggling," one woman said to me, "for God's sake, I beg of you. Don't go anymore!" As a member of the group of relatives, she said this to us. "Please don't go! Listen to me!" We've all been left in a state of fear about continuing our struggle to find the missing.

How would the women in your situation respond if there were an investigation, or a trial, or if they find a body?

More than anything there is a bitterness against those people who have committed these injustices. We'd like to go and scream, "You are this and that!" And to cry out against them, "Why did you do this? Our relatives weren't criminals! You let the criminals run free! And you yourselves are criminals!"

Lucas García is free in his grand mansion, on his big plot of land, in his town of Cobán. And the other, Donaldo Alvarez Ruíz also is away from here and is doing well. Valiente Tellez, too.[12] More than anything, that causes rage. One wants to bring this out, and say, "We know very well that you were the ones! What did you do with our relatives?" But you can never do that, because if you did, the next day you'd show up dead.

No, I don't think that at this point they're going to appear alive. But more than anything, we've been left with this trauma. Oh, my poor children. My son, because of his state, doesn't realize that his

12. Donaldo Alvarez Ruíz was the minister of the interior during the Lucas García regime and is thought to be the intellectual author of many repressive acts. He currently lives in New York City. Valiente Tellez was the head of the Judicial Police during the Lucas García regime and also is considered to be the intellectual author, if not the material author, of many human rights crimes.

father is dead. But he does miss his father. Sometimes he asks, "Why don't we go to papa? Let's go to my papa!" "We can't," I tell him, "because he is far away. You have to take a plane," I say, "and it's very expensive." And my daughter has been affected, as I have as well. My nerves are out of control from so many problems. I feel it's this thing that one keeps inside. Yes, it is talked about, but it doesn't reach the appropriate ears. They are the ones responsible for all the things that have happened—so many orphaned children, suffering children. What blame can possibly fall on these children?

Since this book is going to be published in the United States, is there something you would like to say to the people of the United States who read this book?

In all of these situations, the military wins. They are supposed to be protecting people, but it's not that way. They do just the opposite. For example, the armed security forces supposedly exist to protect citizens, and they do just the opposite. Here in Guatemala there have been military governments, and they have committed barbarities. Now that there is an electoral campaign, they are lying so much. That makes me angry. There are still ignorant people who believe the lies they promise. Perhaps in the moment the promises are made one is without shoes, and since that party is giving away shoes, one affiliates with that party. More than anything, you do it because they are giving you a pair of shoes, or are giving away something that you need. They take advantage of this situation. They go around offering so many things: "I'm going to lower gas prices." "We are going to support union organizations." But all these things are lies.

These are things that Vinicio Cerezo promised.[13] He said that he was going to be on the side of the poor. And whose side is he on now? Prices on all things, such as gasoline, are going up, and the people cannot do anything. They endure it. It's a very difficult situation.

One has that bitterness, one endures and endures, and doesn't have the right to speak up, to say, "A stop should be put to all of this! Remember that you promised so many good things for the people, and you're not doing anything!"

13. Vinicio Cerezo was president of Guatemala from 1986 to 1991.

One could say these things, knowing, however, that one would soon show up dead. I think that my husband wasn't a union member at the time, but he joined the party of Lucas García. I found the card after he had been disappeared, and I was so angry that he had voted for that man. He voted for him so that the next day Lucas could take off his head! To give one more vote so that Lucas could come to power! And there is Lucas, doing well. And my husband is disappeared. I wish that one day, when there are elections, we the people will not give our votes to anybody. I nullify my vote, because everyone knows that it's all pure lies.

4

ERNESTO

Our Strength Comes from Our Hunger

The Committee of Peasant Unity (CUC) began organizing peasants in the mid-1970s, and the organization came to public light in 1978. The CUC suffered a major blow when several of its leaders were burned to death in the Spanish Embassy on January 31, 1980. They had occupied the embassy to pressure the Guatemalan government to create better conditions for peasant workers. Despite that loss, workers on the southern coast engaged in a massive strike to force a wage increase to 3.20 quetzales a day (then the equivalent of $3.20, but now $0.63); this minimum wage remained the same until 1988, when it went up to 4.50 quetzales a day. In 1990, the minimum wage was increased again, to 10 quetzales a day (about $1.80) and in 1994 to 14 quetzales a day (about $2.05). The Ministry of Labor admits, however, that only about half of farmworkers receive the minimum wage.

The CUC's activities from 1980 to 1988 could be described as semi-clandestine. Then in 1988 the CUC began to have a public presence in demonstrations and the press, and it received active public support from various union organizations. Still, it cannot operate in a totally open fashion because of repression in the countryside.

Plantation workers live and work under the most inhumane conditions possible, similar to slavery days in the United States. In 1989 and 1990, coastal workers engaged in CUC-led strikes seeking better working conditions and an increase in the minimum wage to 10 quetzales per day. Both attempts were brutally repressed by police and military forces. In addition to these efforts, the CUC denounces repression against the peasant population, supports the efforts of the Communities of Population in Resistance in the mountains of Guatemala, struggles for land redistribution, and organizes against forced participation in the paramilitary Civil Defense Patrol and forced military recruitment.[1] It was also involved in the organization of continental indigenous resistance to the five hundred year celebration of the "discovery of America" in 1992. There is a strong relationship between the peasant movement and the labor movement; the latter used its strength to back up CUC's return to public life and offered logistical support during the campaigns to raise the minimum wage.

We interviewed a male and a female member of CUC who, for obvious reasons, could not allow their names to be published. They make it clear that it is inhumane living and working conditions that give rise to popular organizations and not foreign influence or "outside agitation," as the government and army would have the public believe. The interview with "Ernesto" follows, and the interview with "Camila" is presented in Chapter 6. Ernesto now works with another organization but continues to do peasant organizing.

---

1. Communities of Population in Resistance or CPRs (Comunidades de Población en Resistencia) are groups of Guatemalans who fled the military repression of the early 1980s but chose to remain in hiding in the mountainous regions of Guatemala rather than leave the country. They were often accused by the army of being guerrilla sympathizers and thus were targeted for bombings. Since the early 1990s, the CPRs have maintained an office in Guatemala City, and several delegations of human rights activists have visited them. The CPRs are currently fighting for recognition as a civilian population and for compensation for damages they suffered as a result of the war. Civil Defense Patrols were created in the early 1980s by the Guatemalan army as part of its counterinsurgency campaign. Mostly indigenous men ages eighteen to sixty serve shifts in these patrols, which provide the military with free day and night surveillance in rural communities, informants about all local activities, cannon fodder for combat, and a means to control any local opposition without a formal military presence in these communities. Although a provision in the constitution states that the patrols are voluntary, many people opposing forced participation in the patrols have been threatened and assassinated. Numerous international human rights organizations, including the UN human rights monitor sent to Guatemala, have called for their dissolution. At the time of this writing, about one-half million men serve in the Civil Defense Patrols.

How did you first become active in the CUC movement? How did you become conscious?

I will have to go back many years to answer this question. During my adolescence, when I was about fourteen or fifteen years old, I was very active in youth movements. However, the story doesn't start there; it starts earlier in my life.

My family wasn't so badly off that we lacked food every day. There were tortillas at home each day, although perhaps not salt. But there were other families who didn't even have tortillas. What they earned on a given day determined what their family ate that day. We were a family of gardeners and managed to get by, though our diet wasn't good.

My father took us to visit poor people, so poor that you felt pity for them. We gave them something, with a feeling that comes from the heart. We gave with a Christian mentality, which begins to form in childhood.

So I have been inspired by those experiences and by literacy work and other activities that I undertook with youth.[2]

Tell us about your work with youth.

Being young ourselves, it was difficult to take on the task of teaching people to read and write. Nevertheless, it was a joy to see so many people wanting to participate, wanting to learn with great enthusiasm. We had many, many people wanting to learn to read and write, and we managed to get a few notebooks and pencils for them. When we saw people's enthusiasm, we paid for supplies from our own pockets.

When you see that excitement among the students, you become interested and enthusiastic yourself. You see people grow. You see them learn at a very rapid pace. What may take years to learn in school takes only three or four months with tutors. And when they are able to read and write, it makes you even more enthusiastic.

But our objective wasn't just for people to learn to read and write. We wanted to awaken the people, to help them learn what to do in

2. According to governmental statistics, 52 percent of the population over fifteen years of age is illiterate. The illiteracy rate among rural residents is 70 percent.

A group of peasant workers prepare the land for sowing. Photo Derrill Bazzy

the face of their situation. We wanted to share what we had learned in school and wanted to know more about their experiences. We had the opportunity to listen to people who spoke eloquently about their situation, who spoke to us in clear terms when given the opportunity to be heard.

I remember from that age on, we got the youth together. But it wasn't easy at first to get young indigenous women involved, because there is a belief among many parents that young women should remain at home. One of the beliefs of indigenous people is that daughters need to be looked after so that nothing bad happens to them.

Therefore, it was very impressive to us that the people had so much trust in us with their daughters. I taught them to sing and to read and write. We learned about their culture. There was no discrimination. There was no desire to isolate people or to make them feel inferior. Rather, there was an interchange. This experience made me grow quite a bit.

You worked with both youth and older people?

Yes, but at different times. For example, we worked in the afternoons with the young women of fifteen or sixteen years of age. Later, at five o'clock we worked with the young men. Following that, we worked with the older people.

In the mornings, I had to work with my father. I worked my father's land. I had to be out very early, at six o'clock in the morning, and work until noon. But by four o'clock in the afternoon, I was with the people.

I owe a lot to my father because he taught me empathy, that concern for others. We could say that all my enthusiasm and interest had its roots in my father, who is a natural leader.

He is part of the history of our town. He helped to establish cooperatives and has been active in Catholic Action and various improvement committees.[3] He founded a radio station. My father is illiterate and never went to school, yet he has presided over various organizations and associations. He has been a radio announcer, even though he never attended school, not even for one hour.

---

3. Catholic Action is a national organization of the Catholic church that combines religious activities with community service on behalf of the poor and needy.

My father allowed me to do all this because I wasn't doing anything bad. I received a lot of support from my father. When I worked with him on the land, I told him that it wasn't really like work because we spent the day talking as we worked. It wasn't a typical father-son relationship. Usually the relationship of a father to a son is one of domination. In my case, it was more like we were brothers. We talked about many important things with ease. We'd go deeper and deeper.

I could say that my questioning began there, with my father, but was further awakened by being in the youth movement. We wanted to create something more for the children. We reached out to pre–school age children and learned how to work with them. But the interest comes from seeing how people grow, how they come to trust you, and how they become conscious of their situation at various levels.

In time, we motivated the youth quite a bit. There was a lot of growth among them. The earthquake helped with that, because we could deal with a variety of issues and carry out activities that before we hadn't believed were within our reach.[4] For example, we promoted a collection of funds for aid. We got totally involved in that effort. This was very important, and we made ourselves known among existing organizations and cooperatives.

Because of this involvement, we received access to the authentic authorities—not the governmental authorities here in the countryside but to local indigenous authorities. When they became familiar with our work, they took us very seriously. They called and spoke with us. This was something that had never happened before.

The council of elders called on us. Elders had never had anything to do with young people. They said, "Come, look at this. We want your opinion." And we were barely adolescents!

And that's how things began. Little by little we were forming our indigenous student association. You see, there was a separation of indigenous from *ladinos*.[5] In the town where I grew up, for exam-

---

4. In 1976, there was a major earthquake in Guatemala that affected primarily those living in poorer areas. This event provided an opportunity for many organizations to form, and for people from various popular movements to strengthen their relationships with one another.

5. *Ladino* is the Spanish term used to define Guatemalans who are of European rather than Mayan descent.

ple, the ladinos were on one side and the indigenous on another. There was very strong discrimination and isolation. Over time we worked on the problem of how ladino youth could become closer to indigenous youth.

We also were able to demonstrate our power. We had a radio station. We had different organizations, religious groups, and cooperatives. This scared some of the ladinos, although our goal wasn't to isolate ourselves but to bring together the indigenous and ladino youth.

We organized immense cultural events. We spent no money, because we called the musical groups and they came without charge. The churches lent their benches—they even delivered the benches to us! We had artists, announcers, and writers. We had a desire to see people participating, toward the goals of community development and stronger community organizations.

At that time was it dangerous to do this kind of work?

We weren't in any real danger, because it was literacy and consciousness-raising work. Later on, however, those same activities cost the lives of many compañeros. They cost us exile. Cost us our homeland. Cost us our families. These became the tolls for carrying out an integral task, for this is what we were doing without even realizing it. We didn't know whether we were leaders or not. We did the work as naturally as possible, without wanting or seeking prestige.

Leadership is a subtle process. But later on it was converted into an explosive situation, when perhaps twenty-five thousand of the thirty thousand residents backed us up. Consciousness was much higher, because the peasant population was awakening. Those who had participated with us in literacy and consciousness-raising projects became leaders of cooperatives and church leaders—leaders with a message.

The Protestants and Catholics took a message to the members of their churches. Not the repetitive message of the Bible but their own analytical messages, adapted to reality. That created a strong interest among the people.

I'm talking about the end of 1979. At the very end of that year, we lost a compañero. In 1980, we began to lose others. We began to lose compañeros through kidnappings, and later through assassinations.

We began with a group of nine or ten compañeros; only three or four survived. At that time we weren't part of CUC but rather a youth group. As I said, there was a great interest on the part of the people, and consciousness developed. Our influence in various organizations and institutions was very strong, including among the municipal authorities. Mayors had to ask our opinion to be able to implement policies.

When you began to lose people through assassinations, did you withdraw or continue your work?

No, we continued to work and even more people came and asked us to continue. The challenge had become much greater.

We were so small, and we didn't foresee at all the repression that was to come in 1980. By 1981, the repression against us was much stronger. What we did was form a small organization, and we went underground in various departments and in the city.

We did not want to lose contact with the people, but we had to break relations because it was such a difficult time. They couldn't leave their towns, and we couldn't enter. That was extremely difficult for us. We were obligated to intensify our consciousness, to expand our vision.

We saw that for offering literacy, they kidnap you. For offering literacy, they assassinate you. Why? What is the real reason? One can't understand.

So we analyzed our situation and decided that we needed the support of other people, of another organization. We decided it would be better to affiliate with CUC. Thus, we began to work with CUC because it was a large organization, and we were trying to branch out to other places in the department. This is what the people wanted.

Did your family always support you despite the risks?

I received the total support of my parents. They had to pay a high price for my departure when I went into exile. For example, they had to pay for my housing and food. They helped me a lot. There is a great deal of consciousness in my family. I haven't suffered limitations because of my family. I've had my father's support, my mother's support, my brothers' and sisters' support. I have been able to count on them because they know that it's a commitment on my part and that it's not easy.

Later on, the situation became much more serious. Not only our group was suffering then; people everywhere were suffering. We were pulled into the cyclone of violence against the popular movement. We were burned. They said we were communists. "These are the ones who promote communism, and they must be annihilated!" But we didn't even know where we were going or what we were doing with the people.

The enthusiasm when we promoted a cultural activity had to be seen to be appreciated. For example, to rescue the culture with the crowning of the queen of the fair was something extraordinary for us.[6] In that activity, indigenous people get together and express themselves and say whatever they have to say. To motivate more than twenty thousand people to participate and say what they have to say in their own language was a wonderful feeling.[7]

People became more conscious of what they had to do about their suffering. And the biggest crime we committed was to organize all of those people. "These young boys are dangerous, because they can pull together and organize many people," the authorities must have thought. I can say that was our greatest crime in the minds of the authorities.

And the authorities fell upon us like wild beasts, not just upon us but all of the cooperatives, churches, and other popular organizations. Later on, in my hometown, a priest was assassinated. He was a North American priest who at critical moments had given us support. This aroused more anger among the people.

You spent a period of time inactive after going into hiding?

6. Most cities and small towns in Guatemala have annual town fairs, and among other events there is the selection of a town "queen." In some places both a ladino and an indigenous queen are chosen.

7. There are twenty-two indigenous languages spoken in Guatemala, and recently many efforts have been made to preserve and revive these languages. These attempts at cultural preservation have been made despite strong pressures placed upon indigenous peoples to assimilate, to use only Spanish.

Never, because participation in the movement becomes a part of one's being. One doesn't feel comfortable alone, or doing nothing, or not being surrounded by people. One feels bad.

This work gives you life, because life isn't simply a matter of breathing. Rather, life is what one does to feel a part of the people.

I see all the illiterate people and their suffering. I had the opportunity to learn to read and write. I owe this same knowledge to the people. I have to share it with them.

No, I never became inactive, but at times I could say my participation was reduced. Part of being active is also protecting oneself, being careful.

You have had security problems due to your work among the people?

Absolutely!

Can you describe some of these problems?

The usual persecution. They are looking for you all over the place. With names and photos, they are looking for you.

One time I received a call from Roosevelt Hospital, supposedly on behalf of my father. The caller said, "We are calling from Roosevelt Hospital. You have to come—your father has had an accident. He's here in the emergency ward now."

I almost lost control. I wanted to go to the hospital. However, I realized this might be a trap. Instead of going to the hospital, I sent my compañeros. I told them what they had to do and where they had to go. I told them to look for strange or suspicious people. As it turned out, there were people waiting for me, but my father wasn't there.

And there you have it. One develops a sixth sense about these things and learns. I have great love for my father, but if I had ignored all my security concerns, the result would have been my death.

Later, things became even more difficult. The incident with the hospital occurred at the end of 1980. During 1980, we had lost more compañeros, but the last days of 1980 were much more difficult.

For example, some compañeros of ours who were fleeing, as I was, fell all at once. Six of them. All six at once in Antigua, Guatemala.

Some were found shot dead, not just with a few wounds but with a shower of bullet wounds. Others never reappeared.

We then began to be more attentive to security issues. We had to disperse. We felt totally cornered. We had to abandon the country and go into exile.

Therefore, for a time I left Guatemala. I had to leave the country. Three days after I left, armed men came looking for me. They said they were my relatives, but these men carried machine guns in their bags. The man who later informed me about this was very moved, because I had managed to escape. Perhaps I was not meant to die.

How long were you in exile outside of Guatemala?

Several years. It was an exile but not a passive exile. I had the opportunity to get to know the situation at the international level and to continue to understand the reasons for our oppression. I still don't understand the degree of repression our country experienced. I had to develop myself outside the country, learn more, and contribute to the denunciation of the serious situation in my country. I had to support the struggle here and find my place here.

But how could you?

Through existing solidarity committees and through new ones that had to be created. We had to structure the international work of committees that currently exist and to deepen the commitment, not just at the national level in Guatemala but also with other countries that had similar missions. We had to work to generate an international consciousness. We discussed the fact that brothers and sisters in other countries also were living in difficult situations and that they should be living well. We saw that even in North America, people were strewn on the streets with nowhere to sleep. This was a confirmation of our adolescent beliefs that indeed there was poverty.

Given the conditions here in Guatemala, how did you decide to return?

The decision to return to Guatemala took place *before* my departure. It was not something I thought about from outside the country. The question was not whether I would return but rather whether I would leave for a while and work outside. I can't remain separated from the people here. The commitment that has been generated over time, which previously was in my community and later developed in other departments and the city, allowed me to see things more at the national level and acquire commitments at the national level. And now that I was pushed outside the country, I could become more familiar with my country and make a commitment to other countries in the world. But my primary commitment is with my people; my work with other countries is secondary. Thus the decision was made to return from exile.

You weren't afraid to return?

Afraid of what, if I hadn't committed any crime?

I know what you did wasn't a crime, but there are some people who disagree with us!

Yes, that's true. I am a citizen, and I have the right to live in my country. We have the right to live in our homeland.

Obviously they don't like it, and they're never going to like it. But neither do I like it that they force me out of my country. Mine is a right that is contained in the Constitution of the Republic! But besides that, how can it be that they banish me from the land of my grandparents and my parents? I am living on the land of my ancestors, and it is not possible to banish me.

To deprive them of the pleasure of banishing us, we must get involved, develop ourselves, and defend our land. We must organize. More people have to participate in the struggle for the defense of land and the defense of life. That is what the CUC allows us to do.

We have to recognize that the CUC is an organization with many years of experience. It is part of the struggle of the peasant movement to develop our communities, to redirect economic resources that end up wasted by corruption, and to hand these resources over to the people so that they may build roads and homes and pay for education and health.

The interests of the government and the wealthy are threatened by this. We have become an obstacle to their becoming more wealthy. They don't like this, but neither can we leave our land in their hands, which is what they wish us to do. Maybe in my town they managed to do this, but on a national level they aren't going to get rid of us.

I understand that you are going to continue to work despite these threats and killings. But that means you cannot have a "normal" life. I imagine that you cannot go around like others or have a family. How do you live your life taking into account these risks?

That's exactly how it is. No Guatemalan family now has an assurance of a safe life, whether they are organized or not. You see them lying in the streets, shot for five quetzales. No Guatemalan has his or her life assured. If they don't die in an assault, they die from malnutrition or injustice.

Those who are organized need to know how to live in the midst of these conditions. Of course, we would love to have a stable life! That is what we want, definitely. But we can't develop a normal life because our actions are controlled; we are treated like thieves.

It is certain that we can't have a stable life or raise a stable family. One can form a family with a series of sacrifices, a series of obstacles. However, we believe we are not the first to confront this test. Our ancestors had these same difficulties. They were obliged to hide in the mountains, and that's why you see villages and hamlets that are so isolated and far away. It isn't because people wanted to live that way; rather, this isolation protected their lives during previous governments. So we must continue that struggle.

One of the characteristics of the indigenous population is that with much creativity and with much initiative it has managed to survive. One could say that with resistance, not allowing ourselves to die out, we've managed to bring our culture with us to this moment in time. Mayan culture hasn't disappeared; it isn't relegated to history. Although there is an effort to make it disappear, here we are, the children of the Mayan heritage. Here we are wanting to retain and develop our own culture. For five hundred years, we have been subjugated. This is the reason for our struggle, why we suffer now and can't have a stable life.

A peasant who isn't organized has nothing. Ask an impoverished peasant how many days he is with his family. He spends two or three days with his family, and the rest of the time he is on the southern coast working someone's land as an agricultural laborer or in the capital city selling merchandise in the square. This is a banishment from one's home in an indirect manner. But it is the same repression we are experiencing.

We are looking for ways to survive and to develop ourselves within these conditions. This doesn't mean that we are going to easily allow ourselves to be displaced from our land or our culture.[8] Our resistance right now, where we've been pushed out of our homelands, is to maintain our own culture. We maintain our own customs, and we're pushing for those customs to survive. We may disappear, but there are others who will carry on the struggle.

There are people in other movements who at times feel that they can no longer carry on. Maybe because of hunger, or fear, they no longer have the strength to continue the struggle. So they withdraw or leave. What is it that keeps you active? Where do you get the strength to continue?

Well, strength comes from our hunger. Power comes from that same hunger. We are not like others, who get their energy from eating. In our case it is the opposite: our determination comes from our poverty, the unjust situation in which we are kept.

This is not simply injustice read about in a book; we are living it in flesh and blood. For example, right now we have a group of people in a repressive situation. Yesterday morning one of them was kidnapped. The army is occupying the village, and who knows what they are going to do tonight? I can't run away from this. If I do, it's as if I'm allowing my people to be killed.

The people need you as long as you can be there for them. It's a commitment but not an obligation. It's a commitment that emerges from within oneself. A voluntary consciousness.

How can our lives be endured? Never getting enough sleep. Resting as little as possible. Eating only when there is time. Never earn-

8. There are an estimated 100,000 internally displaced people in Guatemala. These are people who were forced to leave their homes because of violence and have settled elsewhere in the country. Since 1983, displaced Guatemalans and refugees returning to Guatemala from Mexico, Honduras, and other countries have been placed in army-controlled "model villages" in the countryside. The general term for regions in which several of these villages are located is "development poles," with an army structure regulating the activities of the area.

ing adequate money. No one can endure this. Nevertheless, we survive. And we develop and grow in the midst of all this.

I know that you are preparing to organize on the coast, where agricultural workers represent some 60 percent of the work force. The agricultural sector is the least organized one. Why has it been so difficult to organize agricultural workers in Guatemala?

A major objective of the rich, the government, and the army is for people to remain unorganized so that they can't demand their rights. If we ask ourselves who the workers are on the southern coast, they are none other than the people who come from the highlands. And if we ask ourselves what the population of the highlands has suffered, we know that's where the greatest weight of the repression has fallen. Therefore, the southern coast is the key focus for the peasant movement, and the peasant movement has been the most affected by the waves of repression since the 1970s.

Since the beginning of this decade, there has not been a solid organization because of the dispersion of the population. We realize that with the displaced, with refugees, with widows and orphans, it's not easy for peasants to be approached. Or perhaps they are organized but their participation has dropped. At this time there are major efforts to organize the peasants.

Where does your hope come from after having seen and lived through so much injustice?

Hope is in the population, a population that is not silent, that hasn't been intimidated. People in the midst of their hunger, in the midst of the repression, want to join the struggle. I see this in the villages and in the hamlets. People have nothing to eat, and if one says to them, "Let's struggle," they are going to struggle.

We've seen such important steps taken, where people have developed so much. Where changes have been made in living conditions. Where we have the opportunity to give them something concrete—a social or agricultural project, for instance, that allows them to emerge from that situation.

Yes, it's possible to make changes, yet difficult in the midst of these conditions. There is no security in their lives. Through force they are absorbed by the economic system, and within a short time they are stuck on the southern coast. You see them selling their land because another child has died and they have to bury him or her.

We are trying to get to the root of these problems. The hope is in these people who don't rest day or night, who trust their own ability to organize. To see all these people who have hope in their own organization and are coming around more and more all the time gives us energy to continue. We feel more committed all the time. That is, in a very practical way, where we have centered our lives.

What should be the role of the international community, those people who are going to read this book?

I think that at the international level, and even here in Guatemala, one should not view these problems as a soap opera or get stuck in regrets. Rather, one must become involved. Live it a little. See it at closer range. Commit yourself to participating in some way. Turn this situation around to find life, because what we are looking for here is life. If one is indifferent, one takes a step toward death.

Some may say, "I'm going to participate. I'll give ten dollars or five dollars. That's enough to do." How can one feel at peace in his or her conscience with this response? If we think of the lives of human beings, do they have a price? There must be a commitment that is much greater, thinking of humanity in general. And with that, a larger organization where one can truly participate.

If someone hasn't become organized as yet, it's because there is a lack of interest. They are well off. Their children are in school. The family has medical treatment when its members are ill. They have jobs. They have everything they need. They have all the time they need to rest and even take vacations. Why should they worry? Yet if they see the speed with which this crisis is growing, and if they become organized right now and offer solidarity, perhaps later on they will realize they were organizing to save their own lives.

This is happening. I think the level of poverty and the living conditions in North America have been deteriorating. We can see what is at the heart of the North American economy at this time. The United States does not produce much on its own. It brings much of its raw material from developing countries. What would happen, for example, if Third World countries no longer had the possibilities to provide cheap labor? Or if natural resources became depleted?

Therefore, our brothers and sisters in other countries should think about who is indirectly feeding them. They should concern themselves a bit more with those people, because those people also have the right to live like human beings, to give a pill to their child who has a stomachache, to send their child to school.

Many of our brothers and sisters around the world are Christians. The Bible says that people should help each other and love each other. But in what sense? Who was Christ in his time here on earth? Jesus was a person who was in solidarity with his people, a person who lived with and was concerned about his people. Thus, to be a true Christian, one must concern oneself with all who are suffering, those who are crying blood.

People should have a greater commitment and work in an organized fashion. And that is what the CUC is trying to generate now. Solidarity committees. Organized hearts in solidarity.

I believe that now we must rescue life for human beings. We must see the extreme backwardness in our countries. I don't refer to backwardness on the part of the population but to the mental backwardness among the owners of capital. They don't want to give even a little to the workers who produce that wealth. They pay the workers with death for organizing themselves.

These people don't have a culture. It's a backwardness in every sense: technological, psychological, everything. In this country there are people who lack development as human beings. The only thing they think about is themselves. That is what we must begin to change.

So we think this information should go outside of our country. People in other countries of the world should open their eyes. We have built-in limitations for achieving that, however. We don't have immense publicity mechanisms like those of the government. Many people think, largely because of the information published in Europe, that the current and previous regimes in Guatemala have been good ones. They think that the government has respected human rights and has taken into account the large indigenous population—more than 50 percent of the Guatemalan population is in fact indigenous.

But if the indigenous have survived, it is because they have learned through their struggle how to resist. Struggle has maintained our people. It will continue, as long as there is even one existing Indian. The struggle will continue as long as there is poverty. The struggle will continue as long as there is hunger and misery. Other countries in the world can be assured of this. In Guatemala, the struggle will not be abandoned.

Only when hunger abandons us will we abandon the struggle. Only when injustice abandons us will we abandon the struggle. Then we will enter into a struggle for development, because in the long run what we are seeking is progress and development. The program we want will take place in the diet of the peasants, in the education of the peasants, in health care. It will take place for the poorest of the poor. And not for just peasants but the entire Guatemalan society.

Real development is not for only a few. Our struggle is for social justice, social development. The countries of the world can trust that we will continue the struggle. If one person abandons the struggle, it is because that person reached the limits of his or her participation. But it doesn't mean that the struggle has failed. We are hoping for concrete efforts from other countries in solidarity with our struggle.

A final question: How old are you?

I don't know where my documents are. My age is the biggest war secret I have! I'm old, and my back hurts a lot!

5

MERCEDES SOTZ
and JOSÉ SOTZ

The Land of the Eternal Massacre

The case of Mercedes Sotz and his son, José, has gained widespread publicity through its promotion by Amnesty International. It is a tragic story of an assassination attempt on the father, a municipal unionist, that resulted in the injury and paralysis of his three-year-old child as they strolled through the campus of the national San Carlos University in 1986.

The facts of the story have been well documented by Amnesty International and Human Rights Watch. What we add here is a look at the aftereffects of this cruel and repressive act: the inability of Mercedes to find work because of his public denunciations of the attack; the insurmountable costs involved in José's care; the fact that José's older sister has to work to help care for him and cannot enjoy her early adult years in a normal fashion; and, as always, the fact that justice was never carried out against those responsible for this violent act.

One might expect both father and son to be inconsolably bitter, depressed, and angry about this experience. On the contrary, one finds them to be sweet, soft spoken, firm yet humble, and in the case of José, full of life, humor, and curiosity. One wonders what kind of life awaits him in his adolescent and adult years, in a society that does not have the same economic and social resources for the disabled as other countries do.

Mercedes's method of not allowing himself to be beaten down is to continue to speak out about his story. Although he knows that this will not enable his son to walk again, it is the closest he can come to bringing about justice in a society that will not take on that task for itself.

————————

I am grateful for the invitation to participate in this book of oral histories. Many people in Boston know about our story through the television and newspapers, but now others will know, too. Here in Guatemala, the denunciations against governmental violence that I made last year in Boston have had repercussions. I received an anonymous threat following those remarks about the government, political parties, and businessmen who manage the majority of workers. I don't know who sent the letter, but it said I shouldn't make any more declarations to foreigners. They know me, and they know I was involved in unions in Guatemala, and they said if I continued to speak out I would be disappeared. But we all run risks.

When was this threat made against you?

That was in October of last year.

When did you begin your activities with the municipal union?

I began to work with the labor movement in 1971. I entered as a union member. Then in 1978 I became a member of the consulting committee. In 1979, when I was elected to the executive committee, I took on the responsibility of secretary of technical issues. In 1982, I was elected finance secretary. Later, we held another election and we won again.

Sometime later, internal power struggles occurred within the union. Because some unionists weren't willing to accept the fact that we had won the election, the outcome was contested and the Ministry of Labor became involved. We remained in office while the Ministry of Labor was deciding who won the elections.

Afterward, in 1986, we called for union elections. Arzú became mayor of Guatemala City, and Vinicio Cerezo became president of

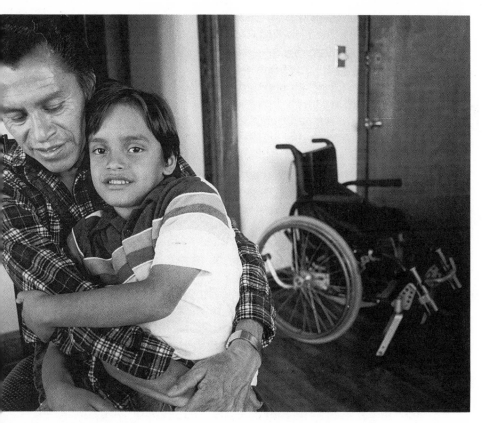

Mercedes holds his son José in his lap, as José's wheelchair awaits him in the corner.
Photo Derrill Bazzy

the Republic.[1] The two, the mayor and the new president, took office, and we were leading the municipal union organization.

When Arzú came into office, he wouldn't have a dialogue with us. Although we demanded that the municipality's personnel regulations be respected, they were not. When we complained that the rules weren't being upheld, the government canceled our monthly pay and we didn't receive our salaries.

We went to the Ministry of Labor hoping that it would intervene. It did not. We then realized that the president of the republic had entered into a pact with the mayor to destroy us and our union. We went everywhere, but there was no intervention. We even spoke with the president, Vinicio Cerezo himself. We asked him to intervene, but he said he could not do so.

We met with the minister of labor, Catalina Soberanis, in her office, but she refused to intervene. Soberanis is a member of the Democracia Cristiana (DC), the Christian Democrat party. We said to her, "We know about the DC. Every four or five years, you take photographs for propaganda. You say that you are going to improve the situation for workers, for peasants. Yet we see in this moment that you are refusing to do so. That means you only want our votes every four years. We will not fall for that lie anymore. We now know who you are. Once we thought you were going to bring justice, but you will not. The mayor is from the extreme right, and you must have the same ideas he has. Right now we are demanding justice and you are denying us justice. We aren't going to believe in the DC anymore. You haven't helped us at all. Where can we turn? We are legal union leaders and you are refusing us. We are going to have to denounce this as best we can." At this point the conversation ended. We didn't shake hands. We didn't even say "thank you" to her, the minister of labor.

We then had to endure a year of working for the organization without receiving one cent of salary. Thanks to other labor organizations that helped us, we did have some support. We asked them to collaborate with us, and they did, but not for very long. The workers were afraid; they didn't want to support us. They were pressured by the administration, the bosses, the mayor, the municipal police, and the National Police.

1. Alvaro Arzú was mayor of Guatemala City from 1986 until 1990, when he left office to run for the presidency. He was elected president in 1996.

We didn't have enough to eat in our homes, and after a year we had to abandon the struggle. We didn't have anywhere to turn. So we said "goodbye" to the compañeros of the municipality, and each one went his own way to see what he could do. We wanted the union to be respected, and since it wasn't, we had to leave it.

Only the union leaders were denied their wages?

We as union leaders were denied our wages, but workers who supported us in the strike also suffered. They were fired. Some were given their benefits pay but not in the way the personnel regulations require, which is one month of pay for each year worked up to a maximum of fifteen months' pay. Many compañeros were supposed to get fifteen months' pay, but they only received seven or eight months. They were cheated of all those months of pay. The mayor made the arrangement so that the workers would be paid less than they deserved, while we, the union leaders, weren't paid a cent because we were a headache. So we had to abandon the union. They destroyed, or semi-destroyed, us.

When did you begin working for the municipal government, and what led you to join the union?

I began to work for the municipality in 1962, but from 1962 to 1970 I didn't know about labor organizations. I was a worker who didn't know anything about my rights. But in 1970, I joined the union because I realized that only by being organized could workers change things. Only by being organized could we ask for a salary increase, be given time off, and receive other benefits. Only by being organized would the dignity of each worker be respected. Only the union can enforce our rights. Without organization, the administration doesn't give benefits as required by the Labor Code. We need to be organized for the future of the Guatemalan people. Prices rise on clothing, shoes, food, and other things. While prices are constantly rising, salaries are going down. We realized that we had to protest against the Ministry of Economy and the government.

When we organized a strike, all of us went out: the unions of Cavisa, Coca-Cola, Sitraincasa, Incatecu, Fegua, Fasgua, CNT. Now there are other leaders, and they have worked slowly because one can't move too fast. So at that time the movement was growing and progressing. The movement helped us become aware of our rights. Only by being organized could we fight for those rights. When there is no union, each political party that comes to power in the municipality does what it wants with the workers. But when there is a union, there is respect. They don't touch us. We began to learn that the struggle is beneficial for the working class.

Although we were in the leadership of the municipal union, we also had to reduce our activity, our militancy, because of Ríos Montt.[2] One time when a group of labor leaders was in his office, he said to us, "If you ask for a salary increase and there is no money, where is the mayor going to get it? Who is going to give him the money? If the mayor doesn't solve your problem, I can cut off his hand. But I also can cut off your arms!"

That is what Ríos Montt said to us in the National Palace. My compañeros and I couldn't say anything. It was clear that if the municipality and the union didn't resolve the negotiation, we were going to have our arms cut off. What could we do? There wasn't anything that the mayor or we could do. The mayor had to get additional money, but he was refused. He was told there was no additional money.

My activities in the labor movement helped me to meet many people from other organizations. In 1983, for example, the national postal service union ignited a struggle. But the union was almost destroyed by the government, by Ríos Montt and, after the coup d'état, by Lucas García. There were always problems, and little by little the labor leaders fell. Many had to leave when they saw that members of the army came to power and that the movement couldn't achieve anything.

There are others whom we met and worked with. An excellent lawyer advised the CNT. He and some others were good people. They

2. General Efraín Ríos Montt, who came to power through a coup d'etat, was president of Guatemala from March 1982 to August 1983. The 1985 Guatemalan constitution contains an article that prohibits anyone from becoming president who previously had ascended to the presidency through a coup. Supposedly this article was written with Ríos Montt in mind. Montt argued that the article said he could not be president, not that he could not be a candidate, but he lost the legal battle to run in the 1990 election. Montt became president of the Guatemalan Congress in January 1995, however, and a surrogate unsuccessfully contested the January 1996 presidential election, losing to Alvaro Arzú.

gave us courses. They were our professors. We received labor education courses from another lawyer, the daughter of an army officer, Yolanda Urizar Morales. However, she was killed when she returned from being in exile in Mexico. She was captured in Escuintla, and she never reappeared.

These deaths are examples for us. Union organizations are very beneficial when the leaders are progressive, when they don't accept money to sell out the organization, when they don't accept a better job while the rest of the workers stay behind. Lately, some leaders can't seem to do anything for their compañeros, because they have received something. They have been bought.

We were called in to see if we would accept certain privileges, but we didn't accept anything. And that's why Mayor Arzú called us friends of the devil. However, we didn't ask for anything, and we didn't accept anything. We always demanded respect for municipal personnel regulations, for the Constitution of the Republic, and the Labor Code. But these laws were violated.

Have you been active with other labor unions, too?

Yes, with Cavisa.[3] There's a compañero with Cavisa who is very active, but many others are no longer here. Some are in exile in Costa Rica; others are in Mexico. I don't know where the rest have fled.

I got to know one a bit, a member of the Coca-Cola union. He was almost killed, but he fled from his car and left. He was an excellent compañero, but to this time we don't know where he is.

We want to have a relationship with other unionists because lately we are alone. I just give thanks to God that the compañero Rodolfo Robles was put in my path. He has done very good work, very beneficial for the workers. The government knows about him because here, on Channel 11, they reported on Rodolfo Robles's trip to Washington. When he went there, he asked at a meeting that neither arms nor money be sent to the Guatemalan government because it only serves to destroy the people. I thank God that Rodolfo is such an excellent compañero. Hopefully they aren't going to kill him, as has happened to so many of us.

3. Cavisa is a glass factory that has had a militant union since the 1960s. After a six-month plant occupation from January to June of 1990, the workers were forcibly removed and the union was destroyed.

At this time I must be careful. When I meet with certain compañeros, I remind them to be careful and to exercise so they can run fast if necessary. For that reason, and no other, I go out running in the morning so that I can try to escape if they come after me. I always leave at different hours, sometimes at five o'clock, at six, or seven. I run a different route each day, and when I go out I always run against traffic. The same when I come back. I am always careful on the road. These are some of the ideas of the compañeros, of the teachers we had in 1978.

Why do you feel the need to be so careful?

Because José needs help. He still can't defend himself alone. He needs someone, and I have to be there. If I'm not cautious, he would be abandoned. There isn't anyone else. My daughter is still working, and she has responsibilities now.

Possibly within six months, or within a year, we will go to Boston. I am thinking about proposing this to my family because it is impossible to live here. I can't obtain work. I have learned a lot about unions that could be beneficial; these ideas should be shared with other workers.[4]

Can you tell us about the time you were captured?

We were trying to get the internal personnel regulations of the municipality upheld and twenty-seven compañeros reinstated who'd been fired without justification. On February 5, 1986, at about four or five o'clock in the afternoon, we all met. I left the office after the meeting and walked on Bolivar Avenue and 21st Street, past 20th Street, crossed Third Avenue and arrived at 19th Street, where I was to take my bus to go home.

At the corner where I took the bus, three people surprised me. They had a car parked there. There were four of them: three grabbed me and beat me, and one drove the car. One hit me in the stomach and the others kicked me. I fell to the ground, and they kept kicking me. They put me on the floor of their car. They took

4. Mercedes and José are now living in Boston, where Mercedes is working and José is studying. José's mother and sister remain in Guatemala.

me to the inside of a building, but I didn't know where. During all this time they didn't say anything to me.

Later on, as I lay on the floor in this building, they began to walk away. They walked a short distance, and then they turned and said that we unionists should let the mayor do his job, and we weren't letting him. They said that if we didn't quit the union, we would pay the consequences. I didn't say anything. I was lying on the floor, and they went away.

Who knows what time it was or where I was? I didn't hear any noise after that so, gradually, I got up, touching to see where I was, since it was dark. I touched the wall, and I stood up little by little. I was searching to see if I could find a door. After going around the room I found a metal door. I thought, "They must have left me locked in. Now I have no way out."

But thanks to God, I found the door to a small passageway. I figured it must have a latch. I found it, pulled it, and the little door opened. When it opened, I saw the street. I saw there was no one on the corner, so I ran out.

At that moment, I didn't feel the pain where they had kicked and beaten me. My eye was swollen, but I ran because I wanted to escape. This is why I said I'm grateful to the compañeros who gave us that course. They taught us to run in a zig-zag fashion, not straight ahead crossing streets.

I reached a place, I don't know where, and found some people. I asked them, "Where am I?" "You are near Mixco," they said. "What road can I take to get a bus to the center of the city?" I asked. They told me to go down one more street and to the left, and walk all the way up.

I began to look in my pockets to see if I had money. I had about 2 quetzales. When a bus came, I stopped it. I had a handkerchief in my hand covering my eye. I got home about three o'clock in the morning and went to bed.

The next day, I sent my daughter to tell the compañeros what had happened to me. I told my daughter to tell them they should be careful and that I wanted to speak with them.

That day, the compañeros of my union denounced my five-hour kidnapping. They got an official municipality car, and they came to get me. From the union office they called the Teleprensa news station, and I told the story. I recounted that I couldn't tell who the kidnappers were, but they were well-armed civilians who said that if we didn't follow their advice, we would pay the consequences. We held the mayor responsible for this action.

I didn't pay attention to my compañeros who said I should stop my union work. Some of the other compañeros said, "Let's keep going in the struggle!" I said, "Fine. We are conscious. If they kill us, they kill us for demanding our rights, for defending our compañeros. They'll kill us for saying they aren't respecting the personnel regulations, which are sanctioned by Congress. They don't respect them."

That was in February. February, March, and April went by. On May 31, a Saturday, a friend who is also a member of the union had invited me to his house. I took my son, José, with me. He had awakened early that day, and he and I were playing ball. I told José, "We're going to visit a friend." So we left the ball in the garden, and I took him with me. I didn't imagine what was going to happen: during the afternoon they shot at us.

We believe they were part of the municipal administration. But it's also Vinicio Cerezo's fault, because he couldn't control the repressive apparatus. On June 2nd or 3rd, it came out in the Prensa Libre newspaper that I had been shot at. But José was the one who received the bullet in his spinal column.

In this town, they say that Guatemala is the land of the eternal spring. But the truth is that Guatemala is the land of the eternal massacre. No government is going to respect workers' rights. No government is going to progress so that one day people can live in peace. We believe that this can't happen unless the United States stops sending more weapons here and unless they stop sending more money.

Here, people have to work. We have to liberate ourselves. We must do it. Yet nothing is going to be resolved because those who have money want more and more profits, while the worker is paid nothing. We want to work. We don't want anything handed to us. We are used to working, but we want to be respected. We can't let it go, because we know there is a law that backs us up.

How has your family been affected by everything you've been through?

The truth is that it is very difficult for us. My family is not content because they feel the loss of my not having a job. Only my daughter is working. From time to time, with the help of friends, I get some work. Thanks to the doctors for whom I was working last year, I earned a little money painting houses.

However, my family is sad when I go to work. They don't know if I'm going to come back. I didn't tell them that I received that anonymous threat because, if I tell them, they will be more scared.

When I was in Boston, it was revealed where I live in Guatemala. One night, some people came to my house, and they were knocking and knocking on the door. They tried to open the door, but it has a chain. The door is tied shut because there is no lock. My family was worried. But I imagine this was done just to intimidate me. Maybe they will do something and maybe not, but I have to stay alert in any event.

I think that someday they may enter the house and attack me. They can come and go as they please whenever they wish. But I have faith in God. For now we are going to be here, in Guatemala. But if God is willing, we will go again to the United States to find medical help for José. I'm not a politician, but I know that we might get political asylum. Here I am ashamed to always ask for help from the union. I want help from other sources, because I know the unions here are also poor. They don't have anything, and I don't have possibilities for work. I have to see what I'll do.

Why can't you find work?

Because they won't give me work. Last year I worked at most for three months. For a while, I worked cutting cloth for bedspreads. But when my employer found out that I had belonged to the municipal union, she said to me, "Look, I think I have too many people here, so your work is going to end. There is work here, but only for those who sew. For you, there is no more work." She just kicked me out, and I was denied my severance pay, my bonus.

When a worker knows the labor laws, employers don't let them keep their jobs because they say they're going to organize the people, show them how to work and what needs to be done.

I told my co-workers, "I'm leaving. May God be with you. Continue working, and respect each other, because you are worthy of this work. Don't let them take your bonus away, because this is mandated by the government. When the owners want to take away the bonus, ask them why. Go to the Ministry of Labor to see if they are going to take it away in other companies."

I said that, and I left. They said, "Thank you for the suggestions; no one tells us these things." This teaching people is a form of consciousness-raising. The companies are that way. They give you a bonus for a while, and then they stop. They don't give you any more.

How do you maintain hope after all you have seen and been through?

Well, I always have had, thanks to God, a relationship with the compañeros, and I have hope that one day things will get better.

Recently we met with a candidate for mayor. He said, "I know you. You are members of the municipal union. I know what has happened to you. I'm not going to fight with you. You lost your jobs because Arzú was your enemy. But if I am elected, and you have been good workers, you can organize a union. There will be no problem with me. I will give you the freedom to organize."

One can say many things, but the proof comes later. Still, we have the hope that life will improve if he is elected mayor. If he doesn't win the election, then we definitely won't have access to our jobs, or to the Christian Democratic government.

Someone who works for the municipality invited me to come in, but when I got there he said, "I want you to join the party." I told him that I was very sorry, but I wouldn't join the party. When he asked me why not, I replied, "What I want is a job. If you give me a job, you should give it to me without my having to join the party. I am a member of the municipal union. I can't get anywhere with political parties. What I want is to work, to earn a few cents with the sweat of my brow. I do not want to sign a book for a political party. "If you demand that of me, I can do it. I can sign. But what will my compañeros say after I leave the leadership of the union? How can I sign a book to get a job? No, I can't accept your offer."

This may be the only way to get a job, but, as I said, it isn't a good idea to work with the government. We've had some struggles with Vinicio [Cerezo], with the Ministry of Labor, with Arzú, with their people. The bosses, the other companies that are united with Arzú are supporting him in his political campaign for the presidency, so we don't have access to him anymore.

There is work in some small companies, but because they are small they pay very little. In one company, I earned only 100 quetzales every two weeks, or 200 quetzales a month, but I have to spend 100 quetzales every two weeks for diapers for José. Nothing is left for my other expenses. And I must pay for three buses; that's 60 cents each way, or 1.20 quetzales just for buses every day. There is no money for food, or for the house. There is nothing left.

How old is your daughter?

She is twenty-five years old.

She has helped out a lot?

Since I stopped working in 1987, for the past three years now, she has been sustaining the household. She buys the food. We hadn't been paying rent, thank God, but now we must begin to pay 70 quetzales a month. Besides that, she needs clothes. I don't even have that for her. She is with us; she hasn't gotten married because, if she were to marry, we would be left alone. I don't know how we would be living now if she had gotten married. But thank God, she is still with us, working for us, for her brother.

What kind of work does she do?

She works as a bookkeeper.

Given the human rights situation in Guatemala, how can the labor movement grow?

I think the labor movement can grow only by making an effort with the rest of the Guatemalan workers. But it's difficult. There is little labor leadership in Guatemala. Most leaders have no knowledge, and the majority of the compañeros are afraid. More than anything, they fear being infiltrated. Many no longer want to be union members. Even to affiliate with a union causes most workers great fear. But to be a leader and to lose one's life . . .

As I said, there is fear on the part of many compañeros. If there were leaders who had a clearer conscience, that would be better. If we were in a workplace where there were six hundred or seven hundred workers, we'd have the capacity to orient them to unionism and to unify them. To teach them their rights.

But with the little knowledge that many compañeros have, it is difficult. The only way it could be done, I think, would be if people like us went to the rescue, calling upon all of those who aren't afraid to join the union. When we were leading the municipal union, two or three of us at a time would go before two hundred or three hundred workers to talk. And when we felt more capable, every one of us took on more responsibilities. We went alone to talk to the workers. We were no longer afraid. This is what is needed at this time, so that the union organizations can grow.

Aren't you afraid at times?

No, because as long as one is in a large workplace, the other workers will defend you. But when there are only a few workers, there is a greater risk of being captured. There is no one to protest on your behalf. That makes one take a step back at times.

A union should publicize itself to make its work known. What the leaders are doing. What their responsibilities are. What they hope for others. What the road to the future is. And leaders must prepare others for a change in leadership, although there are few labor leaders now.

We can see that a lot of work needs to be done on behalf of human rights. The truth is that labor organizations aren't struggling just for the moment, not only in response to the high cost of living. We are struggling for human rights, which have not been respected. We are denouncing the massacres and that people have had their land taken from them; they are forced to live in army camps. People have been forced to abandon their homes and flee to the Mexican border.

The people in the highlands have been hit hard. Peasant rights are not respected. Although the army says they aren't obligating people to participate in the Civil Defense Patrol, peasants are pressured. The army says, "If you don't want to be in the Civil Defense Patrol, it's because you are part of the guerrillas." But peasants work from six o'clock in the morning until six o'clock at night—twelve hours of hard work. After working, they take their hoes and the bit of firewood they carry on their backs, and they go home to eat something. And then they must go out and serve in the Civil Defense Patrol. If someone doesn't go, they know where he lives. They can go pull him out in the night and make him disappear.

Do you think unions can respond to these problems?

Yes, because as people we are brothers and sisters. Now I am here in the capital city, but I know the peasants, because I worked for a long time in the countryside. They should be respected, and unions have to play a role; we have to create unity with the peasants so that they have rights.

Peasants work hard. They sow their crops. However, they don't have plantations. They don't have anything. What they sow and reap barely lasts them for the year. They don't have a salary. When they want to buy a pair of shoes or clothing, they have to sell the little bit of corn or beans that they have harvested to obtain money to be able to buy these things. And their children are unable to study.

Peasants must have the right not to be obligated to belong to the army. Why do we have an army? They are supposed to be looking out for the people, not ordering them into the Civil Defense Patrol. Who is the army defending? The high-level officials, those who have plantations, who are sleeping peacefully. These people aren't bothered. It is the poor person who is bothered, who has nothing, who barely passes through life.

When I was in the municipal union, we always denounced attacks against our peasant brothers and sisters. They are paid less than anyone else. The minimum wage is 3.10 quetzales. That won't feed a family. It's not enough. So this is the fundamental part where we must be allies and ask that their rights be honored.

There is another issue, I think. We need people like you. Amnesty International plays an important role in human rights. Their people come to see how we are doing, because our human rights are being violated. The government does not allow us to organize ourselves, and that is part of human rights.

How old are you, Mercedes?

I am fifty-three.

I felt a little ill when I returned from Boston, maybe from the change in climate. When I came back the first time, I was very thin and worn out. I don't know how, but, thank God, little by little I am getting better and I have the spirit to continue to struggle with the compañeros.

[The interview switches to Mercedes's son, José, who is seven years old.]

José, what can you tell us about Boston?

The last time I went to a room where there were a lot of toys! I stayed a while in the room, and then they took me to the airport. We got the airline tickets, and we went on the airplane. I sat in a seat of the airplane, and I looked down when we were flying and the wings were moving!

You didn't get scared?

Yes, I did! I got chills!

You saw the clouds?

Yes, so white, really white. My papa told me if I grabbed some clouds in a glass they would disappear.

At the hospital, they wanted to know if you had progressed. What did you tell them, that everything was OK?

Yes.

Are you using those leg braces to get around, or the wheelchair?

This is the orthopedic apparatus that you can attach crutches to and walk. Today they're going to put them on in my house.

Are you studying?

No, but my mother registered me for school.

Are you going into first grade?

Yes, next year I'm going to start school.

Is the school near your house?

No, it's kind of far.

And how are you going to get there?

I don't know. Maybe my papa or mama will carry me, or I might go in the wheelchair. As you know, there are a lot of stones at my house, and I might fall from my chair.

Are you going to watch the soccer games?

No, I like baseball. I like the Red Sox! I went to see a game in Boston. I stayed for the whole game. I didn't see who won, either the Red Socks or the Mariners.

There's not much baseball here in Guatemala.

No, but what about American football? I've never seen that game; I've just seen the ball.

Have you seen football on television?

No, but one person throws himself on top of another, and another on another. It's a round ball, and they throw it.

Is this the first time you will go to school?

Yes, next year will be my first year.

Are you going to learn to read and write, or do you already know how?

I know a little—some letters. I can write i, a, m, u.

How do you spend your days at home?

Playing, or watching television with my sister. I have things to write with, and I draw. I made one drawing for my father and one for my sister. But I don't have enough paper, just a blackboard for making drawings. I have different colors: white, blue, purple, yellow, and some others. I have lots of colors, some in boxes.

And other children come to play with you now because you have lots of toys?

My friend Rosita comes to play with me at night, after she makes the beds in her house, in other houses, or in hotels.

Are the drawings in your house? Can we see them the next time we visit?

I don't have paper. I don't know who used it up. I made many drawings, because in the United States there was paper, lots of it!

6

CAMILA

The Only Path Is Organized Struggle

Given the fact that the women's movement is just beginning to take hold again in Guatemala, it was only recently that women began to re-emerge as leaders in many popular organizations. Groups that evolved among the indigenous population in Guatemala have a different history however. It is a strong part of Mayan culture to involve everyone from the community in activities, including men, women, children and young adults, and elders.

Camila's story is this: An indigenous woman trapped in a traditional marriage and gender role is invited to a special training session or meeting where her leadership skills and qualities are recognized. Eventually she is forced to choose between her organizational ties and her family, because her husband does not share her values. She bravely opts for following her heart by continuing her organizing work, even though this places her in both economic and physical jeopardy. The ultimate test of Camila's commitment is the desire of her young children to leave home and join her peasant organization as more active members.

Camila shares with us her development as a young woman, her path toward consciousness, and her eventual leadership in the Committee of Peasant Unity (CUC). Her story may seem remarkable to some, yet it exemplifies the growing role indigenous women are playing in the struggle for justice in Guatemala.

More than anything, Camila's story echoes the point made by Ernesto in Chapter 4: It is not "communist" indoctrination or outside ideology that leads a people to struggle, but simply the recognition of the injustice in their own lives and in the lives of those around them.

———————

How and when did you become active in the movement? Did your involvement begin with CUC?

When I was a young girl, I didn't have a home. This was because from a very young age we were left without a father. My mother couldn't support us, so my sister and I went to work as housekeepers. I began working when I was seven years old. Therefore, I was unable to attend school. I can speak Spanish now, in addition to my indigenous language. This is because I needed to learn Spanish while working in other people's houses.

There I felt discrimination, always. I felt it since I was little because where I worked was very different from what I was used to. Everything is separated between indigenous and ladino. When one is indigenous, they view you with disgust and mistrust.

But I didn't understand anything—why this discrimination existed, why we had this experience, why we were poor. I didn't understand why there were rich people, why there was so much injustice. I simply did not understand.

I got married when I was fifteen years old. I had my first child at sixteen, and, by the age of twenty, I had three children. At that point my husband and I didn't understand each other, and I felt desperate.

There was a time when I wanted to turn to evangelism, and I even spoke to a pastor. I told him I wanted to accept the word of God. I am Catholic, but I was looking for a way to resolve my problems and thought that perhaps evangelism could do this. I didn't want to continue to go to Mass. I couldn't find any meaning in it. I remember that I used to pray and light candles, seeking a way to eliminate our financial difficulties, which were our most serious problem.

Then, in 1973, a neighbor said, "Why don't you come with us and participate in a course that the nuns in the community house are giving?" At first, I mistrusted the priests and the nuns, because

An indigenous woman and her daughter take a break during a demonstration in Guatemala city. Photo Joe Gorin

with us in Quiché there is a problem. There is a division between the indigenous and the ladinos in the Catholic community. At that time I thought that perhaps it was the priests, and not the nuns, who had encouraged that division, and so I joined the course.

The course started in the month of September, and I have a very clear recollection about the first day's topic. It was what we thought about September 15th, Independence Day in Guatemala. I didn't really understand what September 15th was about, so the topic seemed like a good one to me. They spoke to us a bit about history as we were living it and the conquest of the Spaniards. I began to hear how things really were. The nuns asked us if we were certain that we felt free. I realized a contradiction within myself, and I said, "No." They clarified things for me because the 15th of September applies only to the rich, and we continue to suffer.

The courses were offered by the church every three months, and I started to participate regularly. That's where I began to feel that life was worth living, because there was so much to learn. But I never thought about struggling, just about learning.

Then I began to participate more actively. At that time, I also began to have problems at home with my mother-in-law, with my husband, and with my sisters-in-law. They said I was no longer a housewife and that men were advising me. They began to mistrust me. However, I was calm. My conscience allowed me to feel calm, since I was learning with brothers and sisters, friends.

After a while I attended even more courses, although it was a sacrifice to leave my children. My husband didn't understand what I was doing. He never understood it.

I began to realize how one should behave. The nuns spoke of personal dignity, of liberty. They taught that each person is a human being who should be respected and who should respect others.

I also met some compañeros who were collaborators in Quiché, collaborators of the CUC. They didn't say they were in the CUC, but when I was introduced to these people they invited me to participate in a course given by the CUC.

I decided to attend, even though I didn't know what the course was about. As it turned out, one of the topics was literacy. Another topic was discrimination. Later, they invited me to attend other courses, about the laws of the republic and the Constitution. There I realized that laws existed. I had been ignorant about all that.

The courses continued, including one about the national reality. I also joined a group whose only participants were women, and I attended courses given by the nuns at the community house.

The CUC compañeros gave us some tasks in the consciousness-raising course. We had to give literacy courses to others. We went in groups, but I didn't know that an objective was to organize people. Later, the people who were meeting said that they had been active in political parties, cooperatives, and religious organizations. Since I had also experienced that, we discussed it and saw that the problems of society weren't resolved within those organizations and institutions. "Let's form our own organization!" I was listening and also participating. That's where we analyzed and discussed the need to form a peasant organization.

What problems did you want to confront that were not being resolved through other organizations?

Our compañeros were members of cooperatives and were trying to resolve our problems pertaining to fertilizer, insecticides, tools, and how to cultivate some plots of land better. However, we saw that these cooperatives were in the hands of the government, and they couldn't resolve our problems.

Many of our compañeros are involved with banks—for example, BANDESA.[1] They go there to resolve a problem, but they end up worse off because of being in debt. They have to put up the little money they have and then pay interest, so they end up at times without their plot of land because it is seized by BANDESA.

There have been other institutions, such as the Alliance for Development, that were going to teach us about development. But this is not a solution, because these institutions are designed to neutralize us. They give us a piece of candy, but that piece of candy doesn't satisfy us. It doesn't resolve our problems.

That's how we came to see that these organizations were not the way to change our reality. Our grandparents, our parents, and even we ourselves have placed our trust in elections. We all have hoped that perhaps a certain party will win and solve our problems. We

---

1. The BANDESA (Banco Nacional de Desarrollo), or Agricultural Development Bank, offers loans for agricultural activities.

have voted for the MLN, we have voted for the Christian Democrats, we have voted for all of the parties.[2] Yet when they get into power they forget the people. Only when they are campaigning do they say, "We will give you this. We are going to do that." Once they are in power, once they form a government, they are at the service of the rich, at the service of the army, at the service of imperialism. And we sink deeper into our problems.

We were clear about this analysis, and in response we tried different types of activity. Many in the religious realm had been charismatics, Protestants, Catholics. They celebrated Masses, burned incense, to try to resolve things. But that is not the solution. The solution is to unite, to organize ourselves, and to struggle. That's how I began my involvement in the CUC.

What happened with your family problems when you began to be more active?

The problems became worse. There was more mistrust. After the massacre of Panzos we got together with compañeros to evaluate the situation and to plan a strategy.[3] My husband's niece saw me with these compañeros, and she told him that I was out with some men. My husband began to mistrust me more; he thought I was out with other men and that I was deceiving him. He became jealous. Also, my mother-in-law said she had never seen a woman go out by herself, since that wasn't the custom. "This is wrong," she said. She said perhaps I was a woman of the street—a prostitute. My sisters-in-law also began to mistrust me.

But my conscience was clear. What we were examining and discussing was important for our lives.

It was also difficult to leave the house to do this work. There is so much work to be done at home when one is a wife and a mother. It is difficult to leave the children. Not being there all the time with the children is hard. But I did get up early to leave tortillas I had

---

2. The MLN (Movimiento de Liberación Nacional), or National Liberation Movement, is an extreme right-wing political party founded by those actively involved in and supportive of the 1954 coup d'état that brought military rule back to Guatemala.

3. In 1978, peasants were massacred in a town called Panzos when they organized to struggle for land. This was the first of many massacres to follow.

made and to leave *chirmolito*.[4] I had to rush to do what I needed to do. My mother-in-law always said, "She gets up early when she must go out, but otherwise she is irresponsible."

I used to tell my two older sons that I had to go out. Sometimes I took them to meetings, although I had to lie to their father about where we were going. I asked the compañeros if it was correct to lie in front of the children. The compañeros said it wasn't a lie but a cover. I didn't understand what a cover was. They began to explain it to me. They said if I was going out to learn, which is a good thing, then my children would understand. If there was a meeting for three hours, I would tell my husband that I had to go to the health center or that I had to visit my sister-in-law. But that wasn't true. My children knew that I wasn't going there, but my husband did not.

One time there was a meeting, and the children and I left the house at one o'clock in the afternoon, and had to return to the house by five o'clock. However, we were delayed, and when my husband saw that I hadn't come home, he went to look for me at the health center. But the health center was closed. He then said that he no longer wanted me to live with him, and that I should leave.

In one respect, he had the right to feel as he did, because I never told him what I was doing. But the reason for not telling him was that he didn't agree with my activities. My oldest brother also had been in the struggle for a while, and my husband would say to me, "You are going the same way as your brother! Why don't you marry your brother!" That is what happened when I joined the CUC.

How did you finally work it out between the two of you?

I talked to him and said, "Yes, I am in the organization." I gave him the bulletins and he read them. But he didn't care for them. Later, he began to drink more. When I saw that he was drinking all the time and being irresponsible about the needs of the household, I couldn't endure it any longer. I thought, "I can't take this life any-more. It's better that we separate and I will be free. I'll see what I can do to support the children, and I'll have more opportunity to

---

4. *Chirmolito* is a typical Guatemalan dish made of tomatoes, basil, onions, and lemon juice.

participate in the struggle." So we separated. I left home and went to live with my sister-in-law.

For three months we were apart. I was willing to be separated from him, but he insisted that I return home. I did return, and he changed some. Earlier when I had participated in courses or in demonstrations, he didn't understand what I was doing. I did whatever I could to provide for my own transportation and my expenses. I saved, little by little. If he gave me money to buy things, I'd try to buy less, or I didn't buy those things at all. Sometimes I didn't eat anything so that he wouldn't realize what I was doing.

I saved, because I had no way to earn a few cents. As I said, after we separated and I went back, he changed a little. He said that the children should go with me to the meetings and demonstrations. He said he would give me money for transportation. So I was more at peace.

However, we lived that way for only a short time, since we had to separate when the repression began in 1980.

You left with your children?

Yes, I left with my four children. It was difficult, but at least the place we fled to at first provided a roof over our heads and we didn't have to pay rent. We didn't have to buy corn because the compañeros sow corn. When I left the house with the four children, I realized that I would have to play the role of both mother and father.

Has it been that way since 1980, or have you reunited with your husband?

Yes, it's been that way. We separated in 1980 and saw each other about two years later. He missed the children, but there was more mistrust on his part. We agreed that I couldn't go back to living with him in the house and that he should make his own life. He had the right to share his life with another woman, and I had the right to share my life.

Did you personally suffer repression, via threats or loss of family members?

In 1980, the massacres began in the villages near Quiché. They were looking for my older brother, so he had to flee. Another

brother, who was conscious of the struggle but not actively involved in it, was kidnapped on May 7, 1980. He reappeared dead
on May 10. He had been tied up and tortured. They broke his skull.

Who would not be afraid at that time? Dangerous people were
controlling the streets. Many people received threats, and the
bishop and the priests all left. The church practically closed down.
The lay catechists had to leave, also.

All of us in the CUC left. The compañeros told me to leave. They
said that it would be better to leave my husband than to lose the
life of one of our children. So we had to flee with nothing; we left
empty-handed.

How old was your brother when he was assassinated?

He was thirty-eight years old. He was older than I, but single.

*How did you manage to survive, leaving alone with four children? How
did you do it?*

When my mother-in-law saw the repression, she agreed that I
should flee. She said to me, "Why did you get involved in these
things? Look what happened to your brother. That's what's going
to happen to you! You should stop doing those things. I don't even
know what you're doing!"

But I told her that it wasn't possible for me not to be active because our goal is to avenge the blood of those who have fallen. But
she didn't understand. She was afraid that while I was there in her
house, people would come and take me away.

When I told my family I had to leave, they asked where I was
going. "Well, I don't know where I'm going," I said. "How are you
going to manage with the children?" "Some nuns are going to
help me," I replied, although that wasn't true. "Are you sure
they're going to help you?" they asked. "Yes," I said, "I'm sure. The
children aren't going to suffer." I told them this so that they would
stay calm.

That is how it was that I left with the children. I ended up in an
unfamiliar place, not knowing the people there, and the people
looked at me strangely as well. I had to rent a house. One house
there cost 10 quetzales, and rain came in during the rainy season.

We had to pay those 10 quetzales, but where to find the money? I went there without a cent.

The children were small; one was less than a year old. That made me sad. But I told myself, "Nobody obligated me to do this, and I'm conscious of why I've done this." That gave me more courage. There were some moments of desperation, many having to do with the children. I remember that some people did give me 100 quetzales to help out with expenses, but no more money came after that.

In our home we were accustomed to living poorly, but it was even more difficult after I fled with the children. I made friends with a woman who asked me why I was in that situation and about my husband. I had to tell her that he left me. She did me the favor of lending me 5 quetzales to buy some mangos and other fruit to sell.

The children and I began to sell a little fruit here and there. At first, I didn't have the courage to sell, and the woman told me, "You have to talk! You have to offer the fruit or you won't sell anything!"

For the first few days I didn't sell anything, but little by little I offered to sell fruit, to make tamales, or to cook corn, and in this way we managed to survive.

During this time were you no longer active in the CUC? Did the CUC fall apart under the repression or were you always active?

I was always in contact with the CUC through my brother. They sent me some bulletins and materials. Thus, I had the good fortune of not becoming disconnected from my compañeros. I couldn't be in direct contact with those of us who were in Quiché, but we did have a form of communication.

We were all full of fear. Once we saw some neighbors from Quiché. We only looked at each other; we didn't greet one another. We were all full of mistrust. Who knows what the other is doing or thinking? So we didn't speak.

Time passed, and the compañeros gradually began to organize themselves. Compañeros who were leaders came to visit us. Our committee formed a commission to attend to the displaced. The compañeros brought us used clothing, since we left our homes practically without clothes. We used the clothing to make *huipiles* for the children.[5] Later on they came to visit us to lift our spirits.

They gave us financial support, and they told us about how our families and friends were doing. There was a time when some displaced families met, and we were able to share our joys and sorrows, to let them know that at least we were still alive and to talk about our family members who had already died or who had been kidnapped. These were moments to unburden ourselves and to be together.

Later, the compañeros got to know us and tended to our needs. Our compañeros were helping us financially, and our problems were being resolved by our committee. They asked us how many of us there were and what our needs were. So, our committee was meeting our financial needs, since we were displaced.

During that time, was the work of the CUC *more or less clandestine, because it wasn't possible to work openly owing to the repression?*

After the repression began, and after we were scattered, there were still some compañeros in the structure. Some had to flee the country, but others came together and discussed problems and what to do about them.

The members were spread out, but we were always together. Yet, as displaced families, we did spend a period of time doing nothing—just thinking about what to do. The committee began to help us financially and to assume new responsibilities. They were always meeting and analyzing what to do next.

But in that environment of so much repression, how is it that you or they could maintain hope, the spirit to continue with strength?

We who were left had hope because we knew that even though some of our compañeros had been massacred, others remained and could escape. We always remembered that the compañeros were there and that they were thinking about us.

---

5. *Huipiles* are the large, colorfully embroided blouses worn by Guatemalan women as part of their native *traje*, or clothing.

We were hopeful also because the CUC was born with the idea that we must always be united in struggle. The only path is organized struggle.

Our slogan is, "Clear head, solidarity of heart, and combative fist." This is the root of all that we discussed. Our responsibility is always to continue forward. Another slogan is, "In the face of more repression, more struggle." We always have had this in our hearts, a confidence in one another that has never died.

The compañeros tried to get us together despite the conditions in which we were living. The neighbors didn't know where we were from or who we were. We had to change our clothing so that we wouldn't be identifiable.[6] We had to change our language and look for a cover for each of us. This wasn't too hard, because from the start we had used those methods to defend ourselves from repression. Despite all this, our hope never died.

You never considered withdrawing from the struggle?

No. In those times of repression, and in the difficult moments when I did not know if we would survive, I never had any regrets. I felt that no one obligated me to be active. I experienced a process of consciousness-raising that developed gradually until it touched my heart.

We have lived in poverty, and we've felt discrimination in our flesh and blood. Someone points it out to you, and you recognize reality. From the very first courses we took, we began to talk about the reality in which we're living. What the roots of it are. So I had hope, I never was disheartened. It was sad, yes, even desperate at times. But it is one thing to be sad and another to drop out.

At the end of 1980, the compañeros told us that the CUC was growing bigger and bigger. They told us that the need for the CUC was constantly growing. They asked, "Doesn't it make you happy that in our home areas, in our beloved land, there are now more and more compañeros?" So they asked each of us if we were willing to return to our home areas.

6. Each indigenous region has its own traje, with distinctive colors and patterns as a means of identifying the origin of the individual. Our interviewee is saying that the CUC member in internal exile had to wear different traje to avoid being identified as from a particular village.

I said, "Yes, I am willing to collaborate where I feel capable of doing so." I had managed to leave my home once because I had problems with my husband and my mother-in-law. But I no longer had those problems.

I started preparing myself to return. I stopped nursing my baby little by little, and I talked over the situation with my children. They were willing to return, because we could not be at peace after what had happened to their uncles. My older brother had been kidnapped; while we were displaced, my other brother was kidnapped, too; another brother, who was working with the CUC, was kidnapped as well. And so we returned.

Did your brother who worked with CUC reappear?

Yes, he reappeared. He escaped from the enemy's hands. But it reaffirmed our conviction to struggle.

My oldest child said, "I'm leaving. If you want to stay here, you can, but I'm going to join the compañeros from the CUC." My smaller boy wanted to go, too, but I wouldn't agree to it because he was so young.

How old was your son when he said this?

He was ten, and the younger one was eight. My older son said he was going to go with the *compañeros*, and he left.

It wasn't hard for you to let him go?

Ever since he was little, it fascinated him to listen to the news about the war in Nicaragua. He was very little, but he was already interested in the news. But when he said, "I'm going with the compañeros," I didn't want him to go because of what I knew about their struggles. One had to walk a lot. The army was nearby. I tried to convince him not to join the compañeros, but he didn't pay attention to me. His leaving made me sad.

Your son went to work with the compañeros of CUC?

Yes.

Since we were displaced from our villages into the capital city, the compañeros asked us if we were willing to go back to the departments where the seed of the CUC was newly planted.[7] Although the repression was still intense, I said that I was willing to return. The compañeros asked us to wait a few months, but my children didn't wait. They left immediately.

The two of them left?

Yes, the eight- and ten-year-old boys. When they returned, they told me about their life with the compañeros. There they don't use names, just "compañeros." And they share so beautifully.

They began to see a different world. They began to see that we must be united, because if the army comes we have to flee. In this way they were organized. When I heard these things, and the compañeros asked me if I was willing to go, I said, "Yes." I was left with just the two younger children. My boys had gone to another place. The compañeros told me, "You're going to have to endure a lot there. The army is going in; they are burning homes. They are burning everything. There are massacres. You can go if you want to, but it is not safe." Nevertheless, I prepared to go, and my mother, who is quite old, said, "I'm going, too!" So we went with several families who were recently displaced. We were once again in the departments, and we were united with other compañeros from the CUC.

When we arrived, I asked what I could do. "I don't want to just sit on my hands. I'm willing to do my part." We did all this as a community, even though we were in the midst of repression. But I was more at peace in the department, because in the city I didn't feel part of the struggle.

We were suffering, but we were all suffering together. I felt better being back in the department, more vitalized to be suffering the repression, seeing what was happening, and deciding what we would do.

The compañeros gave us the task of grouping the parents together and going out to the markets. And we began to carry out social activities.

---

7. Departments are territorial divisions within Guatemala similar to U.S. states or Canadian provinces.

Instead of hiding yourselves?

Yes, because if we hid it would be worse. It was better to take risks and to go out among the people. It has been a great experience, a great education for me. All that I have learned cannot be ignored. The CUC's hymn says we don't believe in laws, governments, parties, or the vote. The compañeros asked us to form improvement committees, to form school committees. Our community came to an agreement and began to open those social meeting places. The compañeros began to prepare a group of us to be teachers. They asked us what task we wanted to take on. The good thing about the CUC is it asks us what we feel capable of developing within ourselves. I said I would like to be able to teach something to children, and they assigned me courses.

The compañeros gave us courses under conditions in which at any moment the army might arrive. But we worked it out, and we were provided courses with materials, with everything we needed. We formed parents' committees, and the children came to school. We began to teach them primary school subjects and more. The popular education methods were very beautiful.[8] The goals were to teach literacy, to raise their consciousness, and to teach Spanish.

We had to be clear about what the objectives were and whether the children were advancing in their studies. We spoke to them in Spanish and in their indigenous language, and in that way the children learned. Then there was another grade, then another grade, and we got to three grades. Then the fourth grade, and there were more children. Those were the first steps.

The CUC puts a high priority on involving women, elders, and children. That approach is very different from other popular organizations and labor organizations. Why is the CUC like this?

Well, we are clear that the political line of our committee is that we all have the right to participate: women, children, youth, elders, Catholics, Protestants, charismatics, others who have no religion, indigenous, ladinos, every ethnic group. Anyone, everyone. There is no difference. Our struggle is not for religion or for a party. Our

---

8. Camila refers to highly participatory methods that place value on the learner's life experience regardless of his or her level of formal education.

struggle is a class struggle, not one of race. We are clear about that. It is our line, and we're not going to just say it and have it on paper. Rather, it is something that is illustrated in action.

Let's talk about the agricultural workers on the coast. Agricultural workers comprise 60 percent of the work force in Guatemala. Yet agriculture is the least organized sector. Why has it been so difficult to organize workers in the countryside?

There are some people in peasant unions. Those that do exist are mostly in places where there are large plantations.

Here in Guatemala there are peasants who are in debt to the cooperatives, to the banks. Their land is mortgaged. This is the group of peasants who go to the coast to work the land. This is the group that is converted into *rancheros* or into *voluntarios* for work in *cuadrilleros*. The *mozo colonos*, semi-proletariats, spend half the year at home tilling their small plot of land. But the little bit of corn they produce doesn't last, so they spend the other half of the year working on plantations.[9]

Because of these living conditions, it is not possible to form an organization that is composed purely of peasants working on the coast. Our committee, the CUC, represents peasants who work the land on the great plantations.

The person who goes to the plantations is the person who knows better than anyone how to plant cotton, how to plant coffee. He knows the best time to plant and to harvest. There is no union organization, but the workers are organized as peasants.

You are saying that because of the nature of the work, some workers are there part of the year and others are there all the time. Some live there on the plantations, others only stay for a time. Is it difficult to organize a group like that, because everyone comes from different places? Despite these difficulties, are there many CUC members on the southern coast?

9. *Rancheros* or *mozo colonos* are agricultural workers who live on a plantation most if not all of the year and receive minimal housing or a small piece of land in exchange for their labor. *Voluntarios* are temporary workers who spend the year going from plantation to plantation according to the harvest season for various crops. *Cuadrilleros* are groups of agricultural workers from a particular town who travel together from job to job for periods of time.

Yes, and also peasants who are in unions—not just in the CUC but also in other organizations that have arisen, other organizations here, on the southern coast. And we are happy to know that other compañero peasants are forming these organizations, that more of us are becoming organized. We are seeking the same objective, so it makes us happy that there are other peasant organizations.

Our struggle as peasants is an economic one. That is why we carry out our struggle on the southern coast. We believe that the CUC is the greatest force existing among the peasants.

The same system imposes injustice on all of us. The problem in the countryside is that six million of us don't have land. So we all have to come to the coast to work. That is the heart of the problem, that we don't have land. We are exploited on the plantations, because hunger drives us to go to the plantations. That is where the struggle is centered every year. The CUC organized the strike of 1980, and the years of struggle on the southern coast has included all the sectors, the rancheros, voluntarios, cuadrilleros, ladinos, poor people, everyone. We're all there.

You must realize that we have managed to mobilize sixty thousand workers. They feel the struggle is theirs. They trust the CUC, although UNAGRO and the government lie by saying that the CUC is an armed group, that it has caused only problems, that it is provoking repression.[10] But the people know the truth, and they trust us.

What hopes does the CUC have for people working on the southern coast? What are the long-term goals of the struggle? How can the problems of the agricultural workers be resolved?

Our goal, as our slogan says, is to get one tortilla more for our children. The struggle continues, and we are never going to tire. We are not going to retreat from our struggle on the southern coast because we know that there are rich people there who exploit us.

We are going to be flexible with our struggle, however. We believe in negotiation. We have spoken with the owners. We have

10. The UNAGRO (Unión Nacional de Agroexportadores), or National Union of Agro-Exporters, is an old association of large, wealthy landowners which was disbanded in late 1990 and regrouped into other organizations.

asked courteously for just wages. We have made demands. But they have not responded. So our long-term struggle must continue. We must continue organizing ourselves. Seeking other forms of struggle. Preparing ourselves more on political issues. Improving our organizational structure because we know there are risks.

There's a great deal of control over the people, and we're clear about repression. What we seek is a resolution to these problems in the short term, because in the countryside we can see that children are malnourished. They eat only twice a day and go to bed hungry. Thus, we see our struggle as just, necessary, and legal.

The owners say our struggle is illegal. How can they not believe that hunger is illegal? That malnourishment is illegal? Children are dying from common illnesses that are easily cured. If they will just concede a little, much will be resolved. But we aren't going to be satisfied with a little bit of coffee and half an egg. Children need shoes, medicine, and much more. The community needs development. It isn't going to be enough if the owners give in only a little.

There have been pay increases on some plantations because of the intense struggle by our compañeros. This struggle has put them at risk. However, they created a dialogue with UNAGRO, an organization that is the heart of the economy. We see that with the force of our struggle, UNAGRO sat down with the UASP.[11] It's not coincidental that the owners agreed to a dialogue, even though it is a dialogue that leaves one desperate. It's a prolonged dialogue in which meetings are canceled and agenda items are left for another time. During a strike, they delay and delay while the workers work and work, until the harvest is over. They want to leave us desperate and demoralize us. They want to destroy us in every sense, to destroy our struggle.

But their ridicule gives us more strength. They ridicule the hunger of our children, and that makes us very angry. We run risks, as do our people in the countryside. That is why we meet and evaluate, why we identify errors. We are strengthened, and our struggle on the southern coast continues. We have a slogan that says, "Wherever we are, we must struggle." Wherever we are, we are constantly in the struggle.

---

11. The UASP (Unidad de Acción Sindical y Popular), or Unity of Labor and Popular Action, is a coalition of labor, peasant, student, and other grassroots groups which was formed in 1987.

7

TOMÁS JOLÓN

We Have Been Called to Struggle

Workers of the Lunafil thread factory in Amatitlán occupied the plant from June 1987 until August 1988—410 days—in a struggle for their right to a humane workday. Some of the workers remained inside the factory gates during the entire time of the occupation, while others remained outside in support roles. Management responded with repressive tactics such as bribery of workers, detentions, removal of raw materials, the permanent presence of private security forces, and the arrival of hundreds of anti-riot police, as well as the construction of a huge wall that prevented workers' families from visiting them during the occupation.

Despite the national and international moral and economic support that workers received, many could not endure such a long separation from their families. Of the ninety-two workers who began the occupation, only thirty-nine remained to the end, and of these only twenty-four were rehired by management once the conflict was settled. The union continues to exist, but management has done everything possible to prevent union growth. That these twenty-four men have maintained their involvement in the union despite the isolation and injustice to which they have been subjected is testimony to their commitment.

In a final blow, management illegally closed the factory in May 1994, leaving unemployed all unionized and non-unionized workers.

Tomás Jolón, one of the union leaders throughout the conflict, describes what led him to participate and the consequences for himself and his family. Tomás is an exemplary union leader to whom many turn for advice and support.

———

How did you begin your involvement in the labor movement? Were you involved in other popular movements before you became involved in the labor struggle?

Besides my work in the labor movement, I've been involved to a limited extent in some other popular issues. For example, I participated in a neighborhood committee for a while, although it was not well organized.

On the other hand, I also spent two and a half years in the Civil Defense Patrol. This experience raised concerns for me when I saw how the peasants were treated by it and the military. But I tried above all to maintain communication with the people and to deepen my understanding of their problems so there would be unity among us. Those of us who make up the lower class, as they call us here, are obligated to unite and to defend ourselves in the face of widespread repression. This repression exists not only in Guatemala, of course, but throughout the world.

During those two and a half years in the Civil Defense Patrol, more than at any other time in my life, I felt an identity with my people. Because of my attitude toward them, I was respected by them but not by the army. You see, I was an obstacle for the army.

Once, the army obligated people to carry out an exercise they weren't accustomed to which was too strenuous for them. We asked the base in Chimaltenango for a written list of our tasks. Although they didn't want to give it to us, our request had its effect, since from then on the army treated people more moderately. So those are the two areas in which I participated, but my primary work has been in the labor movement.

When did you become active in the labor movement?

I first became active in 1979, in the San Antonio factory in Chimaltenango. We tried to create a true union, but we had to struggle against a management-sponsored union already in existence.

Tomás Jolón, Lunafil union leader, addressing a crowd of demonstrators in front of the National Palace. Photo Joe Gorin

We were able to win a salary increase for the workers through a petition we made to the owners. However, we didn't bring the proposal for the wage increase through the owner-sponsored union, even though we were affiliated with that union against our will.

Soon thereafter a problem arose when the company union saw that we were able to negotiate the pay increase. The company union tried to levy a fee on the workers to pay for legal counsel. Since legal counsel had never been used by the company union, we decided to strike.

The strike lasted one and a half days. We were successful in getting the company union to drop the assessment. They also paid us the salaries that had been docked for the strike. This was a triumph for us, and for myself personally, because the compañeros had delegated four of us to speak to the owners about our concerns. They had made me the leader, even though I didn't know what a union was. However, with practice, one learns.

I was only able to enjoy that triumph for a short time, because twenty-two days later I was fired. They sent me directly to the central offices, in the capital city, where they told me I was fired. They refused to give me my severance pay, even though it was very little money and I had a right to it under the law.

I demanded the pay, and I even went to the Labor Inspection Office to try to get it. These officials arranged with the owners that instead of reinstating me, they would immediately send me my severance pay. Fortunately, I got my severance pay in cash; some companies give it to you in the form of the company's product. If this were the case I would have received fabric, which I would have had to sell, probably at a very low price. However, they gave me the severance pay in cash.

Did the company fire you because of your union activity?

That's right.

But they didn't admit this, did they?

They simply said there was no work for me. Of course, the labor inspectors have always had ties with the owners. Consequently, they do very little for the workers, especially in a case like mine when only one person is affected. When a union is involved it's different, because there is strength in numbers.

What happened after you were fired?

Following that, I spent three months working in the countryside. Later I found work in a company in the capital city, but there was no union. Yet there they treated the workers rather fairly. Later, I was laid off from that company because of general economic difficulties. This was another fabric factory; I have always worked in fabric and textile companies.

In 1982, I joined the Lunafil factory. During the first five months, I was not affiliated with the union. Later I had to join because of pressure by the supervisors. When a worker is not affiliated with the union, the managers pressure him a lot not to join it. They also pressure him to work harder and harder. They threaten him: "Avoid the union, or else you'll be fired." Nevertheless, I ran the risk and joined the union. This was beneficial, since the managers stopped pressuring me. I tried to work conscientiously, as was specified in the labor contract, and at first I had no problems.

After joining the union, I began attending union assemblies. Immediately the compañeros wanted to elect me to the directorate, but I really didn't have the knowledge to serve in leadership. However, through my participation in the union I learned more and more until I was finally named secretary of conflicts of the union.

What year was that?

That was in 1985. I also was chosen to serve as a member of the joint labor-management commission for a two-year term.[1] Under rules established by the General Labor Office, each member of the union directorate serves a two-year term. Shortly before our terms were to expire, in July 1987, the occupation began and our terms were extended. The occupation lasted 410 days, and we ended up serving about three years and three months.

---

1. The joint labor-management commission is a group of negotiators representing both the union and the company.

During that time we had to work very hard, because there were many needs both inside and outside the factory. As you know, those who stayed outside had to mobilize themselves to go to the capital city to visit other unions, to receive delegations, and to do other kinds of organizing. Those who were inside the factory had to attend to the visiting delegations and other people who visited us in solidarity.

How did you spend your time during a typical day of the occupation?

During the occupation I wasn't doing very well, particularly in spiritual terms. I had many problems. I saw families destroyed by conflicts. Many workers and their wives came to me to discuss their problems; it was a burden for me to see this and not be able to do anything. One can give advice if there is some to give, and, if not, it's better to say nothing. Yet people aren't obligated to accept advice, and in that sense it was very difficult for me.

Had you spoken with your wife about your union activities before the occupation began?

No. But at the time of the occupation, our neighbors kept my wife informed of everything that was happening in the company. My wife suffered, because she knew what was happening to the popular organizations. This worried her a great deal. It was especially hard for her, because at that time we didn't have family close by; it was just the two of us living there. She didn't have anyone to turn to in times of need.

How many children do you have?

Now we have four.

Does your wife support your union activities?

To some degree, yes. She is conscious of the benefits of unionism because she has seen the gains we've managed to obtain through the union struggle. In that respect she sees unions very positively. What she doesn't view as positively, which is understandable, is that problems can arise for union members and that few struggle while many benefit. She doesn't like that much, but she tries to accept it.

How was your family affected by the 410-day occupation of the Lunafil factory?

It affected them in several respects. Emotionally they suffered, because for a long time I wasn't present in the house. My oldest child failed a grade at that time, something that had never happened before. One of my other children passed with very low grades. This also had never happened before.

In material terms, we all suffered very much, but especially my family. Before the occupation we had many animals—rabbits, chickens, and ducks. But when I returned home after the occupation ended, there were no animals left. The economic assistance we obtained through solidarity efforts were very small in comparison with the salary I'd been earning, even though that salary was very little in relation to the cost of living. Therefore, my family became even worse off. They badly needed clothing and shoes. Financially they were quite affected.

Their health suffered, too. My wife was ill with a nervous disorder and rheumatism, which affected her whole body. I wasn't able to help her while I was barricaded inside the factory. And, to some degree, I couldn't talk to anyone about this problem. One learns to manage this alone, even though there is trust among the compañeros.

In our country it is said that the labor leader is the last to eat, the last to go to sleep, and the first to die. Thus, I seek the well-being of my compañeros, and my personal needs must come last.

Have you had security problems such as threats or surveillance?

The truth is that I've had many problems. At Lunafil, in October of 1986, an unusual thing happened while I was going to work at 5:40 in the morning. Two men approached me. One had a rifle under his jacket, and the other had a machete in a bag. A few others were some distance ahead of us and behind us.

As I was walking, they stood in my path so that I couldn't pass by. The one with the rifle raised it up and put it against my body, ordering me to stop. Their attitude led me to believe that this wasn't a simple robbery or assault: the first thing they did was to frisk my chest and my pants legs, all the way down to my feet, as if they were looking for a weapon. Of course, I had been taught this practice in the military. Then they took my money and my documents. They examined the documents and returned them to me. Then they left—with my money!

Since they were armed and since there was a group of them, I couldn't do anything. But when I arrived at the factory, I told some members of the union executive committee what had happened.

About ten minutes later, although we hadn't said anything to anyone else about these events, the supervisor came in and said that we should be very careful. From this exchange we deduced that this was an event directed by the company. Later, in a meeting of the joint labor-management commission, the threat was discussed, but the company preferred to avoid the topic.

The managers, on the other hand, made it known that they were very much involved in what had happened. They became annoyed when we tried to discuss the threat and told us that there were methods available to fire a union directorate member.

I began to be followed near my home and later, during my trips to the capital city, as well. I've always been under surveillance, with people watching me all the time.

In 1987, at the beginning of the year, I began to receive some anonymous letters. In the beginning they demanded 300 quetzales and instructed me to leave the money in a certain place. I couldn't hand over that kind of money; in the first place, I didn't have it, but also it wasn't correct to comply with these demands. I got in touch with the police, and we devised a scheme by which I would leave a package in the specified place. But no one appeared.

Then they began to leave anonymous letters for me at a neighbor's house, three notes in all. The fourth letter came directly to my own home, and once again we tried to do something with the police. The police and I kept watch on my house at night.

Later they sent me a fifth note and demanded half a million quetzales. That brought me some peace of mind, because I thought these people must be out of their minds! Where was I going to get a half a million quetzales?

The letters never mentioned your union activities?

No, they only asked for money. That's as far as it went. But after that I received death threats against my entire family. Nothing happened to me or my family, but the threat was there. And management was monitoring all of my activities at work.

Later, when we began the strike, the threats became much more direct. The threats came not only from the business owners but also from the Ebano security guards, the National Police, and the regular police.[2] So from the moment of the occupation to now, there has been harassment of me, my family, and my compañeros.

Have the threats continued, even after the end of the Lunafil occupation?

Yes, the threats continue. For example, recently when I was between 20th and 21st Street in Zone 1, a man crossed my path, and I went over to the other side of the road. He continued to observe me, but he didn't dare do more since he realized that I had detected him. But later, men in a blue vehicle at 8th Avenue and 11th Street watched me for a long time and followed me.[3]

Last month, two compañeros and I stood talking by the entrance of the UNSITRAGUA building. A man came closer to hear what we were talking about. When we went inside the building, he followed us. We saw that he was following us, and I told the compañeros that we should go upstairs into the office. At that moment, we saw that there were several of these men. We took precautions and went upstairs.

These things happen fairly frequently. Two months ago, some people told me that I was being pursued because supposedly I work for an organization managing a lot of money. I was told that they wanted to make me disappear for that money. Of course, UNSITRAGUA doesn't have that kind of money. I don't know where they got that information, but that is what I was told.

But your position in UNSITRAGUA is coordinator of finances, isn't it?

2. Ebano is the private security guard company that maintained a continual armed presence during the occupation of the Lunafil factory.

3. Every major city in Guatemala is divided into numbered geographic zones that are part of the formal address of each building. UNSITRAGUA is in Zone 1, the center of Guatemala City.

Yes, that's the name of the position. In reality, however, I don't have much time to be at the UNSITRAGUA offices; I need to take care of the union and my own job.

Let's return to the discussion of the occupation. You began with more than ninety compañeros and ended with thirty-nine. Obviously many had to leave the struggle for personal reasons. In your case, how was it possible to maintain your strength to continue the struggle? How did you confront all those problems you told us about? Aren't you ever afraid? Do you ever think of dropping out of the struggle?

I think that in this life each man, even if he denies it, is sometimes afraid. But my position is very complex. To drop out of the labor movement, to forsake the struggle, is to do precisely what the enemy wants.

We need to continue to struggle not only for our families but also for all those workers who aren't organized. To some degree our struggle benefits all people, because when the unions in Guatemala obtain a pay increase, the pay of other workers also rises—not only in the capital city, but also in the various departments. It wouldn't be fair if only one group got an increase and another didn't; a pound of beans costs the same for all of us.

We look for opportunities to promote the organization of a new union or to be in solidarity with neighborhood and popular organizations. Although organizing is very difficult, it can be done.

The need in our country is great, and only by organizing can we obtain improvements. If you are going to die, it's better that it happen because you're doing something worthwhile. At least there'll be people who appreciate what you've done. At least you'll be remembered. That is the greatest satisfaction in life.

In the case of Lunafil, the struggle ended with twenty-four workers still committed to the union.[4] That was some time ago. Why has the union not been able to grow?

---

4. At the end of the struggle, thirty-nine workers were left, but, as part of the settlement, the company allowed only twenty-four workers to return to work. The group of thirty-nine decided by consensus which fifteen workers would lose their jobs.

This is because of the managerial repression that exists in different businesses, particularly at Lunafil. The owners and managers remain resentful of our union because of all the profits they lost during the occupation.

They wanted to put an end to the union but not to end it in a simple way by firing all of us. No, they wanted to make each one of us suffer. They also started their own organization, a solidarist association. That's solidarity in name only, of course. All activity is controlled by management, and all workers are told that they must join the solidarist association.

New workers on the official work roster were offered 1,500 quetzales as a bonus under the condition that they not speak to any union members.[5] The penalty for violating this rule became clear when a compañero from San Marcos greeted us and shook our hands when we returned to the Lunafil factory. A few days later he was fired for that. New workers, not on the official work roster, were offered a 1,000-quetzal bonus with the same condition: that they not speak to any unionists. The company made a mistake in the quantity of money they offered the workers. They ended up paying out only half of it to the workers.

By the time we found this out, the solidarist association had already been established. Since that time, no one has wanted to join the union for fear of being fired. We understand their fear, because their needs are much greater than wanting to participate in a union. The workers are under a great deal of pressure working in Lunafil within the solidarist association. When they can no longer endure so much work and long work hours, the twelve-hour shifts, they quit their jobs and go somewhere else. But they don't run the risk of joining the union.

We could say they are a bit cowardly, afraid to confront reality by joining the union to see what happens. And in that sense we now have a problem. The collective bargaining pact that we signed when we went back to work is about to run out. We negotiated a three-year pact, and now there is only one year left. According to that pact, we have to present a proposal for discussion four months before the old one runs out, which means we only have eight

5. Workplaces in Guatemala have official staff personnel lists, while other workers are hired only temporarily or on contract. Tomás is referring to the official list.

months left to begin to negotiate a new pact. But we are at a disadvantage, because we haven't reached the number of members required by the law; 25 percent of workers must be affiliated with the union to negotiate.

So that is our major problem. We don't know how we are going to acquire enough members so that we can negotiate. And the solidarist association is not going to negotiate a pact, because the company isn't going to negotiate with itself!

The union can continue, but it cannot negotiate a collective bargaining pact because there are not enough members?

That's correct. There are approximately 160 workers in Lunafil, so according to the law we would need approximately 15 more in the union—at least 40 members—to be able to negotiate a pact.

How do you maintain your spirits in the face of all this?

Well, it is very hard. Financially, for example, we have had problems with our bonuses. The state decreed bonuses for us, but then we were told that it wasn't applicable to us because that decree was ambiguous. On the one hand, they said a bonus of 30 cents an hour must be paid to all workers; on the other hand, they said that the decree is not applicable when there is a collective bargaining pact in existence.

This has caused us a great many problems, and we now see that we can't have any hope. What the company did was to give the increase planned for August ahead of time. They gave 1.50 quetzales to everyone; yet beforehand they arranged to give an increase of 0.40 quetzal a day to all those who are solidarist association members but no increase to union members. Later, instead of the bonus incentive, the solidarist association members were given 9.25 quetzales a week, and those in the union were given nothing.

May I ask how much you earn in a month?

I earn 12 quetzales a day; about 300 per month.[6]

6. Approximately $60 per month at the time of the interview.

Does your wife work?

No, she doesn't have a job. However, my oldest child is already working. He is eighteen years old and lives at home. He works as a carpenter, and although they pay him only a little, at least he is working.

Does the law allow a worker to belong to a solidarist association and a union at the same time?

In theory, one could belong to both. In practice, that person is not trustworthy because he would be playing, as they say, two cards at once. There is another problem, too. Members of the solidarist association have 5 percent of their salaries deducted as dues, and some are already annoyed with this deduction. If they were to join the union, there would be an additional 1 percent deduction for union dues.

But, as I said, this person would not be trustworthy to either the company or to us.

In the Guatemalan context, with all the human rights problems, how can the labor movement grow? Is there a future for the labor movement?

The future of the labor movement is totally uncertain. Last Sunday, for example, we heard the president of the republic speak of his satisfaction with the activities carried out by the army to maintain control in the country and to control all organizations not in agreement with the so-called democratic process taking place in this country. This can be interpreted as all of those organizations that have expressed their discontent with the attitudes shown by the government—including unions.

Cerezo also said in his speech that the control has been directed toward all the leaders of the popular organizations and labor organizations in Guatemala. We really don't know how far they are going to allow us to go. So we make our plans, but we don't know if they're going to allow us to carry out those plans. But, what we do know is that as long as we are alive we will have to struggle, because no one is going to come and struggle for us. We have been called to struggle for ourselves and for others.

Many people came to you to talk about their problems. But did you have someone to talk to about your problems?

That was difficult. All the problems came to me, but mine couldn't come out to anyone.

Are there people who inspire you? Do you have heroes?

There are people who truly have been and continue to be an example to me. And at the same time they inspire a lot of trust within the labor movement. These are people to whom I can turn when I find myself in trouble for lack of familiarity with something. Mostly, these compañeros are found within UNSITRAGUA. There are good people within the labor movement, in the popular movement, and at the international level, too. I have very positive memories of individuals whom I met during and after the occupation—people who took the initiative to support our struggle.

Is there a role within the Guatemalan labor movement for people in other countries?

Yes, there is, and various organizations are currently playing an important role. Their moral support for Guatemalan labor organizations is very valuable. By moral support I refer, for example, to the thousands of notes and letters expressing solidarity during the Lunafil struggle. Thousands of communications were sent from other countries to the government, to the Minister of Labor, as well as to the owners of Lunafil. To some degree, this gave protection to the union, because the government and owners had to think a lot before acting against us. That's not to say that anyone is untouchable; here in Guatemala, an American can die just like a *chapin*.[7]

7. *Chapin* is a slang term for a Guatemalan.

8

CONSUELO PANTALEON

He Gave His Life for the Union

Consuelo is the widow of Rolando Pantaleon, who was assassinated on July 2, 1989. Rolando was a member of the Coca-Cola union. He was active in the union's theater troupe, whose performances highlighted the problems of repression by managers, landowners, and the army. Because they were tall, Rolando and his brother, Flavio, often had to play the roles of the military in these performances. Thus, it is even more ironic that he eventually fell victim to the same repression about which he was trying to educate the population.

At the time of this interview, Consuelo was still devastated by the event and unable to overcome her feelings sufficiently to carry out her role as a mother in the way she would have liked.

When did Rolando become active in the Coca-Cola union?

In 1980, I believe. When I met Rolando, he had been working for Coca-Cola for four years, more or less. Little by little, he communicated to me that he was participating in the union.

Had he been politically or socially active in other ways before 1980, or was his involvement in the Coca-Cola union the first time he was active?

Members of the Coca-Cola union sing their union anthem at a cultural festival in Guatemala City. Rolando Pantaleón and his brother Flavio are in the back row. Photo Karen Brandow

It was the first time. At first he didn't tell me much about what was going on at the plant. He was very quiet about it. It was rare that he would tell me anything about the occupation. Only afterward did he tell me that he was being pursued.

Later, Rolando became active in the Coca-Cola union's theater group, Dos Que Tres. Yes, I knew about it, but I could never go to see him perform because of the children. I had them one right after the other, and there wasn't anyone to take care of them. So I could never go, and I regret that. I thought that there would be a video of Rolando and the theater group, but there isn't.

There is no video of them?

They say there was one, but it was taken far away. I would have liked to have seen it, but it's impossible.

How many children do you have?

Four.

I used to come to the UITA office more often, but my mother missed me. She had broken her ankle, so I couldn't keep visiting the UITA office. But in three months they're going to remove her cast. Now she's like a child, because someone has to take her to the bathroom, bathe her, and prepare food for her. Having to care for her has made things more complicated for me, yet it has helped me recuperate somewhat because I stopped constantly thinking about Rolando. Recently, as the first anniversary of his death approached, I did feel depressed, but this passes.

You said that Rolando told you that he had security problems. What did he tell you?

Rolando told me that some cars were following him to the karate school. But no more than that; he didn't tell me anything else. Maybe he thought I was going to say something.

Two times, people came to our house looking for him. I told Rolando to flee, to get out of the country. But he would never listen to me. "Even if they kill me, I'm going to die fighting," he'd say. But he didn't tell me anything else.

So they came to the house when he wasn't there?

Yes. They came to our house twice. The first time was after my brother-in-law, Flavio, was shot in the ankle.[1] Since Rolando worked in the same company as Flavio, Coca-Cola, they came looking for him, too. But I denied knowing him and said he didn't live there.

Later, Rolando was threatened; they threatened him right here in the neighborhood. But he didn't pay attention to the threat.

What did they say in the threat?

They said that his death was pending. That the dead don't speak. But Rolando didn't pay attention, and exactly fifteen days later, on July 2, they came to take him away.

They made the threat to you or to Rolando?

To my husband. Rolando said they were judicial police. But Rolando didn't pay attention, even though I advised him often to do so.

What did you want to do?

I thought we should change neighborhoods, that he should leave the company, that he should stop participating in the union, because it scared me. I didn't want to lose him.

But Rolando said he would rather leave me than leave the union, and he continued to participate in the theater group. Fifteen days after the threat, they came to take him away. I didn't realize that they had taken him. People came later to tell me that he was dead. I had to go and identify his body.

I didn't know this would happen. He told me hardly anything about the union. Nothing, nothing, nothing. Maybe he didn't tell

1. Rolando's brother, Flavio, also a member of the Coca-Cola union and the Dos Que Tres Theater group, was shot in the street by several men after a cultural event celebrating the fourth anniversary of the Labor Unity of Guatemalan Workers, UNSITRAGUA, on February 25, 1989. Flavio was constantly pursued and threatened after that incident, and he and his family went into exile in August 1989.

me because he didn't want me to be scared. Since I have heart problems, he probably was worried that I'd get sick.

Do you have any resentment toward the union because of what happened to Rolando?

No. But since this happened, I can't look any policeman in the eyes.

On the day they took Rolando away, how did you find out what had happened to him?

About two blocks from where I live, there is a street where Rolando liked to play ball. He always took the children there to play. That day he told me to get them ready because he, the children, and my brother were going out for a walk. When Rolando left, he went out only in shorts. He didn't wear a T-shirt or socks, just sneakers and shorts. A little while later, they took him away. They just put him in a car and took off.

Since my brother was with Rolando, he saw everything, and he chased after them. Then my brother went to the police. I went to the union to let them know what had happened. The unionists mobilized themselves and told me not to worry because they'd look for him.

At five o'clock in the afternoon, men came to tell me that two bodies had been found, one on the Belice Bridge in Zone 18 and the other in Palencia. They asked me how Rolando was dressed. Then they said, "He's the one who was found in Palencia." They told me that Rolando had already been taken to the morgue.

When I went to that room, I was still asking God that it not be Rolando. But when I entered the room, I saw it was him. I found him face down. When they turned him over, I saw his wounds. His cheeks were swollen. And his face had bullet wounds—five in his head. He had been tortured, and his head was detached. It appears that they . . . And he had rope marks, as though they had tied him up and dragged him with the car. All of him from here up . . . His mouth was swollen . . .

I wasn't aware of anything else, because right then I fainted. I didn't speak anymore. I was mute until they took him away. At midnight they took him away from the room, and they did an autopsy.

Did you go by yourself to identify him?

My father and my brother also went. Later they told me how I threw myself on the ground outside the building, how I screamed like a crazy person and how I cursed those who killed Rolando.

And the children realized what had happened. Now that a year has passed, they have been better, but the two boys cry a lot. I find them crying, and they tell me they are crying for their papa. "I want to see Papa," they say, "take me there." And so I take them to the cemetery, and they kiss the tombstone.

Yes, the children cry. They feel it strongly, because he played with them so much; they played intensely. Since he passed away—I don't know if God will forgive me—I've withheld some love from them. I wanted to be alone and not have children. If I had no children, perhaps I would have taken something to be reunited with Rolando. The children have been studying, but now they don't want to go to school. When I take them to school, the teachers tell me that during recess the children cry.

How old are your four children?

One is 7, one 6, the youngest 5, and the girl is 8.

How did you explain to the children what had happened?

The day that Rolando was killed, since it was late when we returned, the children were already asleep. People didn't want me to show them their father, because they would see him all disfigured. But I told the children that their papa had died, and the four of them did go to see him and kissed him. They knew he was dead.

Did they ask why he had died? Who had killed him?

I didn't explain it to them, but they heard conversations. My room is very small; I cook there and they sleep there. Every time people came, they would hear conversations.

"It's true that he was in the union," I told them. A few days later they asked me, "Is it true that some men killed papa? What did they do to him?" And I explained it to them, but my family said I shouldn't tell them what had happened because it would poison their spirits. But how was I going to lie to them? When they grew up, I didn't want them to reproach me.

Now they know where he is buried and everything that happened. I went to put a cross in Palencia. I go there to speak to him. I dream of him, and the children dream of him. They tell me that in their dreams they are playing with their papa. But now they are crying, for days at a time. I pray a lot to God.

How has Rolando's death affected you?

I don't know if I should struggle anymore to go on living. I don't even know what it is that I want. When he died, at first I took to the vice of liquor. I was drinking, and I went to seek help from Rodolfo.[2] I owe a lot to Rodolfo and the other unionists. Rodolfo told me, "When your mother is better and she says, 'I'm going to take care of the children and you go to the office,' you should do so. It is not good that the children see you drinking."

Now that I've stopped, there are still some days when I have the urge to drink, but instead I go outside and the urge goes away. Now I rarely need to go to see Rodolfo.

So you have begun to recover your religious faith?

Yes, now I say that God has alleviated my wound. When I go out for a walk with the children and I see couples out with their children, I feel sad that I was left alone. Right away the children say that I am crying for papa. "No, it's because I have a headache," I tell them. But I don't enjoy playing with them since Rolando passed away. Instead of giving more love to my children—they need more love, and my family says I should give them a lot of love—I'm very distanced from them.

Why do you think this has happened? Why have you become more distant with the children?

I was more giving of myself with them before, you see. I would even stop eating to give them my attention. I took them to school,

2. Rodolfo Robles, of the union UITA.

dropped them off, and picked them up, and I even went to see them during recess. Now I don't do these things. They come close to me and ask, "Mama, do you love me?" And I reply, "Yes my child, but get away from me."

I don't know if it's my nerves—because I'm really nervous—but when they are playing and yelling, I tell them, "Keep quiet! I don't want to hear any more yelling!" This affects them, because their father never told them to be quiet. He never hit them. He was very caring. He even scolded *me* because sometimes I scolded the children. Rolando told me that I should speak to them, not hit them or scold them.

But it's also very difficult to be alone with four children.

Yes, and there was also a time when loneliness affected me, not the loneliness for another husband but loneliness for a friend to talk to. But people here in the neighborhood, people from all over, only come to find out about your life. Then they go around discussing it. So it's better that I keep quiet, although that has done me harm. During the day I am content, because I'm with my mother. I talk to her, and she says, "Don't feel bad, I'm here with you. You're not going to be alone."

When everyone goes to sleep, at first I feel peaceful. But then I begin to feel that horrible sadness. I feel like my heart is pressured. I feel like it gets smaller. I pray a lot to God. I have prayed to Him often.

And have other family members supported you?

Yes, mostly my brother. He works at the Coca-Cola factory. He helps me a lot with the children and with the IGSS.[3] I wanted to work, because I was staying with my in-laws; it's their place. My family home is nearby, but my brother and my father are there. I want to live alone, but my mother says to me, "If you live alone, you're going to grumble about not having any company." But the company that I desire is someone to talk to.

3. The IGSS (Instituto Guatemalteco de Seguridad Social), or the Guatemalan Institute of Social Security, handles national health care and death benefits for a portion of the working population.

And you don't have that now?

No, I don't trust my friends very much.

When Rolando was assassinated, there was a lot of publicity, both na-tional and international, about the case. Did that affect you? Did you have security problems because of the publicity?

Not at first. I'm upset right now, because a week ago I received a threat from a woman, and I went to tell Rodolfo Robles about it. At first I didn't think much of the threat, but more recently, I became frightened. However, I turned things over to God.

A while before that threat, some men were looking for me, but they didn't come to my house. Some neighbors came to tell me; they told me what the men looked like and that they had come in a brown car. These neighbors said that the men had asked for my mother by name and that they took them to where my mother lives. However, the men didn't want to talk with my mother but with me.

So I called Rodolfo, even though he gets annoyed when I don't come to the UITA office in person. (It's hard for me to go to the of-fice. I can't pay anyone to help me with the children. I only get IGSS, money for food.) I told him, "Two men came looking for me, and it worries me a lot." Rodolfo told me, "You can't talk about this on the phone. It's better to come to the office." I was irritated. And I didn't go to the office; I couldn't.

When I saw Rodolfo today, he asked me about the men who came looking for me. "What were they like?" he asked. "I didn't see them," I told him. "My neighbors told me they were tall and dressed like cowboys with boots. They were in a brown car with dark windows."

Then I told Rodolfo, "When my cadaver shows up, you'll under-stand." He was a little upset with me, because that was how my husband came and talked to Rodolfo: "They are threatening me, and they are following me." Rodolfo said all he could do was put in a report to the police. My husband didn't want to report the threats against him, and fifteen days later his cadaver appeared.

If your neighbors tell you that two people were looking for you this week, it was us. We went looking for you on Tuesday.

But that was during the day, not at night. Besides, those men were there for a while, near the market, waiting in the dark. Certainly they already knew where my mother lives. When I walked four blocks down the road to where I live, I became really nervous. I said, "My God, I can't believe that you would also leave my children without a mother!" I began to pray. But since that time I haven't heard anything more about these men.

How have you been able to survive economically?

I received some support, but I don't know from whom. But I received this aid and, thank God, it served me well; with that, I could maintain myself until I got the money from IGSS. But it isn't enough to cover the expense of food, clothing, and shoes for the children. So my brother asks me what I need, and he brings me food or milk, and sometimes he takes the boys out to buy them shoes. But as I told him, I want to work and buy a plot of land, or a little house.

Did the aid come from international people or from the union here?

International. It came three times. However, I owed a lot of money because Rolando left debts. Even though he's dead, they don't forgive the debts. I have a credit card I must pay. This aid has helped me a lot, and I'm very grateful. But now there is only the money from IGSS.

I was planning to work. I was studying to be a beautician, and I was going to work at night. But when my mother broke her ankle, they had to put a cast on her whole leg. And I was the only one who could stay there during the day to take care of her. The rest of the family is very far away, and my brother and my father must work. I sometimes leave her as late as midnight, because she is upset and cries a lot. My mother is tired of being in that condition.

This happened to her about a year after Rolando's death. I told my mother that I would give anything to have my husband be only injured, because then I would have him with me. Although her ankle is fractured, she is still alive.

How do you manage to take care of your mother and the children at the same time?

I take the children with me to her house. She wants me to move in with her, but I don't want to because of my brother and my father. I don't want my children to see the problems that they create. I don't know how my mother has been able to put up with it. I tell them, "I'm going to take care of my mother, and if you keep on this way, I'm going to take her away." But they don't listen to me.

And the Coca-Cola union: has it given you emotional and economic support?

Yes, both emotional and economic support. When Rolando died, the workers of Coca-Cola and those here at the IUF gave me assistance to pay for the funeral and the things I served, food, coffee, and other things. They also supported me later, and I'm very grateful because they helped me even though Rolando no longer worked there.[4] Now that a year has passed, I just held a Mass, nothing else. I couldn't do a commemoration because I had been left without money, and I would've had to provide food for everyone. I still would like to do it, but I need my check to come.

You had a Mass held where you live?

In our neighborhood church, the priest held a Novena for Rolando.

How do you view his death? Was it for a cause or did he die in vain?

Yes, for the union. I like it that he gave his life for the union. He spoke well of the struggle. I don't blame anyone other than the government, since that's where all the problems begin.

You said before that it was difficult for you to look at policemen. Is that because you think they are the ones responsible for Rolando's death?

---

4. Rolando left his job at Coca-Cola three months before he was assassinated, although he continued to be active in the theater group.

Yes, because the men who came to take my husband away were armed. They had long pistols.

Did the men who took Rolando see your brother?

Yes, they saw him.

But they didn't say anything to your brother?

Not at first, because he was behind. Then my brother yelled to the men, "Why are you taking him away?" But they didn't respond. They just grabbed him. One man pointed a pistol and said, "Get back or we're going to shoot you here!" But my brother didn't pay attention. He followed them, and since a great many people gathered behind him, the men couldn't harm him.

If I had been there, who knows what would have happened? I'm capable of throwing myself at those men and hanging on to them so that they couldn't take Rolando away. But many people tell me that would've been worse, because then the men would've taken the two of us away.

Have you pursued an investigation or a trial?

Someone is being investigated. We suspect him. The military prosecutor called me because the suspect was a soldier, and he later passed on to the G-2.[5] However, he doesn't work there anymore. He tried to leave the country, but they didn't let him.

If I were to ask you how you would like your life to be in one or two years, what would you say?

I am confused. I was worse before, but now with the compañeros Rosita and Rodolfo, and all of the compañeros in the union, I'm doing better. They have helped me a lot.

They say I should work, that I should study, that I should distract myself with something. When I was studying, I was relaxed. But then I'd hear songs that Rolando used to like, and I'd get upset.

5. G-2 is the shorthand name for the Army Intelligence Service.

When I returned home and the children were sleeping, I would lie down. Then that sadness, that horrible loneliness, would come over me. Who could I talk to? Finally I would sleep. But at night, I say, "My God, why did you take him away!"

Is there anything else that would be important for people to know, that you would like to communicate to other people, including foreigners?

Recently Rodolfo took me to see a psychologist, and she began to counsel me. But I told her, "With my pain, the life that I live, no one can help me—only God! I ask him to punish those who did this! Why didn't they think about leaving four children alone!"

Rodolfo has talked to me about going to the country where my brother-in-law lives. He said that perhaps there I will forget everything. But I said no, because the injury is one I carry inside. What hurts me most is that because of dedicating myself to the household and taking care of my mother, I don't give my children enough care. I don't give them enough attention. I wish my nerves could be cured, but I must take some tests to get treatment. I haven't been able to do this. My doctor is helping me, and he wants to do some tests on my heart, but I haven't had these.

I have Rolando's picture. I look at it, and I still go to the cemetery. But now that a year has gone by, I have stopped cursing God and damning the assassins.

How many years were you and Rolando together?

We were about to complete eight years.

How old was Rolando when they assassinated him?

He was twenty-nine. I'm twenty-seven now, I was 26 then.

I believe this is a wound that will never heal. The effects are always there. But one has to keep on living, to find a reason to go on.

Yes, they tell me to struggle for my children, but I don't have that strength. Perhaps it is because I don't have anyone's support. That's partly because in my family, two men are alcoholics; my in-laws are evangelicals, and they tell me to accept it. I tell them that I just believe in He who is above, and I don't believe in what the Bible says.

Is there some way to get together with other women who have suffered something similar? Have you had the opportunity to talk with other women who have been through the same thing? It occurs to me that this could help a little—to share what you are suffering.

Many times I went to the UITA office to cry, and Rodolfo has counseled me a lot. In the beginning I never thought he would give me so much help and support.

9

NORMA

Finding Courage
Where There Is None

Norma is the widow of a worker who was assassinated during the administration of Vinicio Cerezo. Instead of turning inward or allowing the situation to paralyze her, Norma shows incredible strength not only by getting a job in the same company in which her husband worked, but also by considering entering into union leadership. There are probably many reasons why one person responds to a similar situation very differently from how others do, but Norma's firmness and dedication serve as an example to all those affected by political violence, as well as to her own children.

———

When did your husband become active in the labor movement?

When I met my husband, he'd already been active for two years, although there wasn't a formal union yet in his company. My husband told me that he and his compañeros had formed a union among themselves. So he was among the first in his company to agree to participate in the formation of a union.

He had previously belonged to a union in the town where he worked. His fellow unionists proposed that he be the secretary general of that union, and he agreed to take on that position.

"Long Live the Struggle for Peace: Women Are Present." Photo Joe Gorin

I didn't like his doing union work, because there are many problems for people active in unions. I'd heard from others about their troubles. In his particular union, my husband was the first to be killed. I suppose that to this point he's been the only one killed. I always told him not to get involved. But he said, "No, I like this work, and I'm going to continue even if they kill me. I must continue."

My husband and his union compañeros didn't approve of corruption. As in most institutions, many times there is corruption in unions. He found out that there were a lot of corrupt people in the union, people who really were agents of management. He didn't like that, since he was the secretary general.

Many people approached him and told him of their problems with management. They were able to remove the previous manager, because not only my husband but everyone opposed the manager. That's when my husband's problems began. Many of the corrupt people in the union also were removed, and within a short time my husband began to receive threats.

The threats against him started in 1988, a year before he was killed. He was a very active unionist; he became the union president. One afternoon, as he was returning home from the union office, he was threatened by three men (former co-workers of his). They told him that if he didn't leave the union they were going to kill him. My husband responded that he wasn't going to leave the union, and if they wanted to, they could kill him.

These men drew a pistol, but the owner of a nearby beauty shop, a neighbor of ours, came out and confronted the men. She said, "Why are you going to do this to him when he hasn't created trouble for anyone?" That helped; she saved him. He waited in the beauty shop for the men to leave. She hid him there for a good while, about an hour.

Afterward, he came home. When he told me what had happened, I said, "Why don't you flee?" But he remained, and the threats continued. They got the telephone number of the union, and, since they knew he went there every night, they called him there and threatened him. They said again that if he didn't leave the union, they would kill him. They told him that they had already tried once, and the next time they would succeed. He paid no attention to their threats.

When did this happen?

These threats occurred in 1988, and he died in 1989.

The Sunday before my husband was killed, he was on his way to the union office when a man on a motorcycle followed him. When my husband told me about it, I said, "That's just your imagination." I was hoping to calm him down a bit. "No," he said, "he followed me for about two blocks from the union office; he was waiting there for me when I left."

The next day, he went to the executive committee and made the threat known. On the following day, the executive committee asked him if he should leave for a while. My husband had attended two labor courses in Mexico. They said, "Why don't you go to Mexico to throw them off track?" He said, "No, I can't, I'm very low on money."

The next morning, Wednesday, he left the house at 5:15 to catch the 5:30 bus. As he did each day, he announced he was leaving and asked me to go out on the street to see if there was anyone suspicious there. I said, "No, just a boy that we know." It was a boy who works on the bus. I told him I'd go with him to the bus stop, but he said, "Go back to bed, it's still early." I did, then about five or ten minutes later, neighbors came to tell me what had happened. I didn't believe it, because he had just said goodbye and left the house.

Who came to tell you?

It was one of his cousins, a young boy. He said, "Cousin, Cousin, they've killed your husband!" I didn't believe it. "It's true!" he cried, and when I saw all the people, I went outside to look. I wasn't fully dressed; I was still in my night clothes. I ran about three blocks from the house, where my neighbors met me. By the time I arrived, he was dead. The neighbors said that my husband was still alive when they sent the boy to tell me what had happened.

I assumed all our troubles would end then, because I thought what they wanted was to eliminate him. It wasn't good for the company to have him working there because he always spoke of the rights of workers. The managers didn't like that. I thought, "It's all over. But what am I going to do?"

Two weeks later, an anonymous threat came to me saying that I would be sorry if I didn't leave the country. I was told that what they had done to my husband, they'd do to me.

That was in a letter sent to your home?

Yes, they sent a letter to me, but I didn't pay attention to it. "I can't leave my home and family," I said to myself." Even if these are *his* family members, they are all I have." I don't have any other family. I only have my in-laws. My mother-in-law is disabled; she can't see.

However, I had to work. Some friends got me a job in my husband's company. I was more or less able to manage because at least I had a little home there. Even if it was small, I had a place to live.

I went to work at this new job. A few weeks later, I was talking to a co-worker, and people later told me that he was one of the men who had killed my husband. Everyone said he was the one.

Members of the union told you this?

Yes, some union members told me. One of them asked me, "If you knew who killed your husband, what would you do?" "Nothing," I said, "because God is there, and He is the one who will be in charge." "Not me," one co-worker said. "If they killed my brother and I knew who did it, I would kill them."

But I don't have the heart to do that, because I have children and I don't want to continue the chain of violence. After my violence would come more vengeance. I'm relieved that my husband wasn't killed for being a thief. They killed him for fighting for our rights as workers. "Isn't that right?" I asked a co-worker. "Yes," he said. "That is what's left for me," I said, "that's why I feel proud."

A short time later, I received another threat in the mail. I showed it to a co-worker. This threat was definitive. It was clear. If I didn't want to die like my husband, the letter said, I must keep my mouth shut and flee the country. The letter said they didn't want my two children to be left without a mother as they'd already been left without a father.

I was afraid. I spoke with an engineer I knew from that town. He told me to go to Guatemala City, or wherever I wanted, but that I could no longer stay where I was. Before I could leave, I had to talk with some friends. I'd been in contact with them before, and they'd found me a job. I told them about the threat. They talked to the engineer about what I should do, and they sent me to Guatemala City. I stayed in the capital city in December and January. Then they arranged a transfer for me to another place.

Since that time, I've been in and near the capital city. But I don't feel comfortable, because being here is not like being in your own home. Even though I'm not paying rent here (because I'm with my sister, who has her own home), I don't want to be here. I want to go back to my town. But they tell me, "No, you can't go back, because the man who killed your husband continues to work there!"

I'm told that in that place there are four men who killed my husband. When he left the house that day to go to the corner to catch the bus, there were four men. There was a motorcycle on one side of the street and another motorcycle on the other side of the street. A bit farther up the street, there was a white truck that they intended to use to kidnap him.

These men knew my husband very well, and they called out to him. "Come here," they said. "No," he replied. "Come here. We're going to take you away in the car." "No," my husband said, "my bus is waiting there and I'm going to get on it." "No," they said, and they took out pistols, because they realized he wouldn't go with them voluntarily. When my husband saw they had pistols, he started to run. When he ran, they shot him and left him there.

According to the accounts of the people who witnessed what happened, the four men wanted to kidnap him—who knows with what intention? But my husband resisted the kidnapping. So, they didn't take him away; they shot him and left him there to die.

Who was responsible for your husband's assassination?

The company. I don't believe any of that talk that it was unionists. My husband told me he got along well with all of the unionists.

The company, and those who are paid by the company, believed that my husband was a communist, or something similar. They called him a communist. They said that he went to receive guerrilla training to intimidate the company.

You said that when your husband began to explain his union activities to you, you tried to convince him not to participate in these activities. Was that because of fear?

Yes, out of fear. I said to him, "We have two children. Stop for the sake of our children." Our children are now six and nine years old. They were small when he became involved in the union. But my husband said no, that he wouldn't leave the union. He told me we had the right to insurance. My husband said to me, "If I die, that insurance is there, and you can ask for it. You can work to supplement that money." But I haven't yet seen that money. The union tells me it's still not ready, and they have me waiting.

As I told my sister, if the compañeros from the union hadn't found me work, I would be in real trouble. I got my first IGSS check a week ago; 100 quetzales for the three of us. Combined with the 100 quetzales I receive from a fund for orphans, that's 200 quetzales each month. A family of three cannot live on that amount of money.[1]

My husband had told me I would need to plan in the event anything happened to him. Since I like retail businesses, he suggested I start my own. "Open up a store," he said, "and with that you can get by." (When he died, I had my store.) But thank God the union found work for me here, and because of that the children and I are more or less making it. It's more difficult now since everything is so expensive, and I'm in the situation of being alone with two children. Even when a husband and wife work, there isn't enough money. We're making it, but now that the children are in school that's another cost. My daughter is in third grade, and my son is in first grade.

How have the children been affected by their father's assassination? Do they understand what happened?

They miss him in every sense, always. Sometimes my sister and her husband visit, and they put the children to bed. This makes me remember that when my husband came home every afternoon, the first thing the children used to do was lie down in bed with him, all of them together.

---

1. At the time of this interview, 200 quetzales equaled approximately $35.

Financially we're making it, but in all other senses they miss him. They miss him the most for his moral support.

Do they know that their father was assassinated?

Yes, they were sleeping with me on the morning he was killed. When the children heard people banging on the door, they got up and listened. They heard the boy, my husband's cousin, say that four men had killed him. When I came back to the house at about eight o'clock, my son, who was five years old, said, "Mommy, they killed my papa, didn't they?" "No," I said. But my son said, "Yes they did! I know they killed him!" From that moment, the children knew their father had been killed.

The truth is that I don't talk with them about it, because I don't want them to feel bad. When our daughter sees his photo, she cries. A short time ago I took her to work with me, where they have a big photo of my husband, and she began to cry. I try to change the subject so she'll forget. Otherwise, she'll cry.

When you received the threats, how did you feel? What did you think?

At that moment, I decided I had to leave there. Some people said to me, "I don't believe they are capable of harming you." My response was, "How can you say they aren't capable of harming me! Didn't they already do it once? Didn't they kill my husband?" "Yes, but he's a man," they said.

I know what those men are like. They're even capable of killing children, let alone a woman. And that's why the first thing I thought of was to come here, to the capital city. When I came here, the unionists asked me if I wanted to flee the country. The truth is that I didn't want to leave, because one runs into many unknown things, and all in a different language! You might need to ask something, and not everyone knows how to speak your language. I said I would rather not leave Guatemala.

And since that time you haven't received additional threats?

No, I haven't received any more threats. But when I visit my brother, who lives next to my house there, two strange men always appear. Once I heard them saying that they were waiting for someone, and until that person arrived they weren't going to stop coming by. I don't know if they were looking for me. Who knows?

Are they there only when you visit, or are they there all the time?

They are there from time to time. I imagine that they want to grab me by surprise. When I go there, I don't give people notice. Let's say I go today to my town. The next day I come back here to the capital city. When I'm in the town, I don't stay by myself. I don't stay with my in-laws, either. I'm afraid. I see that the company is investigating and that the co-worker who killed my husband always asks when paychecks are distributed, "Where is she working? In what part of town is she located?" Since my compañeros know who he is, they tell him that I no longer work there and that I went to another country. But this man keeps inquiring about where I am.

Did you join the union?

Yes, because where I am now the workers have problems. One time when we were talking, perhaps I went too far. I told my coworkers that the union is for us and of us. I said, "I would like to be in the leadership group to show workers how to act. I have enough nerve."

About eight days later, there were rumors that union leaders were going to put me in the leadership group. But I declined. "Didn't you say that you have the nerve?" they asked. "Yes," I said, "but not now." They told me that within two years, they'll put me in the leadership group.

At the beginning of your marriage, you didn't want your husband to be involved in the labor movement because of the risks. But now it seems that you understand a bit more, being on the inside, what workers' problems are like. Is this true?

Yes. My husband used to go to meetings, union assemblies, the Coca-Cola factory, places where there are unions, and to labor courses in Mexico.[2] He told me about what he had learned. "That's why I have more courage," he said. "You don't want to leave the union when you learn how we're treated as workers. The *orejas* can't do much alone."[3]

He told me about the corruption that exists throughout the country, not only in his company but everywhere. Maybe that's why I gradually became more aware. The first time he went to Mexico, I was angry. But afterward I saw that he was right to go to the labor education courses. Now that I'm working, I see even more that he was right.

And are you seriously considering entering the directorate in your area within two years?

Perhaps not, because there are rumors that the company is going to fire me.

Why?

I can tell you this: It's not easy to get along with everyone. The company resents my requests for time off. That's why I had to think a lot about seeing you today. I didn't want to ask for the day off, so I only asked for two hours. Since I'm on the payroll list there in my town—that's where my paycheck is distributed—every two weeks, on payday, I have to ask for two hours off to pick up the check. We usually leave work at 4:30 in the afternoon; on pay day, I leave at 3:00. The company says that I get too much time off. You would think that this is a right we all should have, to get our checks. So for that reason, I may not last long. More than anything I'd like to return to my town, because I never had work problems there. But the compañeros tell me it's not safe for me to go back.

We have seen people who have suffered the same problems that you have, but who don't have the strength to continue. They don't manage to find the spirit to overcome their problems. How do you find the strength to go on?

2. The Coca-Cola union is one of the strongest in Guatemala, as a result of a successful fifteen-month occupation of the plant by workers from 1984 through 1985. This struggle received national and international support from unions, churches, and other groups.
3. *Orejas* (literally, "ears" in Spanish) is the slang term for informants or infiltrators.

As they say, hunger makes one . . . And the children give me courage to continue. There are times I don't have courage for anything. But I ask myself, "If I stay here sitting on my hands, how am I going to manage with the children?" God and the children give me courage. The children have to eat, so I must find courage where there is none.

When my husband was assassinated, I didn't think about having to find a job. I thought only about the pain I was going through. Others think about the future. The unionists here, all of them, came to see me. My sister-in-law, my husband's youngest sister, asked what possibilities existed for my finding work. Within a few weeks the unionists came again and said if I wanted to work, they could help me find a job.

I told them, "I don't really *want* to work but I *have* to do it, I have to work. Look at my children. I have to push ahead for them, not for myself. I must push ahead for them."

I was in no condition to work, but I had to. I was extremely depressed. I wasn't thinking at first about what I had to do for the children, how I was going to feed them. I wasn't thinking about anything except their pain. Who knows where one gets the strength to go to work? Somehow I am surviving and pushing forward for the children. I can't say we're surviving very well, just more or less, even if it's only with tortillas and beans.

Apart from the support the union gave you in finding a job, have they helped in other ways?

I used to visit the union offices often but not since the threats started. The union just called me and told me that they had been speaking with the president of Guatemala about my case. The union is insisting that things not be left this way, that those responsible for my husband's death be captured. The president told them he already knew who the assassins were, but he wanted one of us—preferably me—to accuse those four men.

I told the union, "Look, I'm not even doing anything. I'm minding my own business, and they are harassing me, threatening me. If I publicly accuse them, they would have to kill me." But the president told the union that if someone didn't denounce these killings, things would never change.

In the beginning, the union did everything possible so that those responsible for my husband's death would not remain unpunished. They made pictures, posters, many things, beginning on the day he was killed. They made a picture with a slogan. I have all of those papers.

Even the police were involved. One time the police chief in my town stated that the police already had the names of those who participated in my husband's assassination. They identified four men, but what was lacking was someone to go and accuse them. The police couldn't do anything with just the names. But nothing has been done, because we can't risk going to the police with an accusation.

You haven't gone to the police to identify these men because of fear, so there has been no arrest, no trial?

Those men are there working peacefully in my town, while I am in constant fear here in the capital city. If I had my own home I would be more relaxed, although I have no problem living with my sister. But I believe that one shouldn't have to depend on other people. We must depend on ourselves. My sister gives me a place to live and other help, thank God. She and her husband have been very good to me, but it isn't right to remain in this situation. That's why I want to go back to my home, but my sister and the others tell me I shouldn't think about it.

Given the circumstances, you don't have much of a choice. I understand your desire to be independent, but on the other hand you have to protect your life.

That's why I've held back and stayed here in the capital city. More than anything I've done this because of the children, because they'd be left alone if I were killed, and that's not fair. However, they aren't happy here, and they want to go back to our town.

Because their friends are there?

Yes. Also their grandparents. But we can't go back.

10

RODOLFO ROBLES

Hope Never Dies

Rodolfo Robles was launched into national and international fame when he found himself in charge of the historic Coca-Cola workers' occupation of the factory in 1984 and 1985. Despite this fame, everyone describes Rodolfo as one of the most humble, open, and accessible labor leaders in Guatemala.

He works long hours, and the doors of the Guatemala International Union of Foodworkers (IUF) office are always open to anyone. The work of the office extends far beyond its mandate to serve only foodworkers, and the office has promoted interchanges with Salvadoran unionists, a committee of women workers, a health clinic for poor and unemployed unionists, and cultural projects.

Rodolfo has been subjected to constant threats, surveillance, and a brief kidnapping, yet he is unwilling to abandon the struggle or the country. He still serves as a member of the Coca-Cola union's advisory committee and participates in union assemblies. His interview provides insights into his leadership style and the unusual way in which his family has been involved in his work.

Other interviewees refer to Rodolfo as the key person offering them ongoing support and advice. He is committed to keeping victims of anti-union or violent repression from falling through the cracks. There are few leaders like him in the country, and we offer special thanks to him for his help in arranging several of the interviews that appear in this book.

———————

Please explain to us how you began your involvement in the labor movement. Had you been active in other movements first?

Very few people know this, but before I became active in the labor movement I was involved in the student movement. From about 1964 to 1967, I participated at the rank-and-file level in the secondary school student movement. Then I was involved in an organization called Catholic Youth, which later was dissolved because its leaders were assassinated. In secondary school, at the Adrian Zapata Institute, I participated as a rank-and-file member of various student groups .

Later I worked more formally in a company called Libreria Hispania, where the majority of us were minors and our salary was approximately 48 cents a day. We worked from seven o'clock in the morning until eleven o'clock at night. We put together a small movement, even though we were very young. This was about twenty-five years ago. We opposed paying social security taxes, so we went on strike, even though most of us were minors. Finally we were fired. So you could say this was the first time I was involved in the labor movement.

Later I worked in various activities, sometimes in private companies, other times on my own. One time, about 1963, I worked for the government in the General Office of Road Works. We were working on the construction of a road in the northern part of the country. We worked for fifteen days straight, twelve hours a day, although they paid us for only eight hours; they never paid us for the four overtime hours.

The work was practically militarized. We worked in the quarries with dynamite, so the project was under military control. Since there was no union organization among the workers, we organized a movement to address the problem of our wages. We finally were able to get payment for the four overtime hours that we worked each day.

This was, in fact, the second time that I participated in a union-type activity but without being organized. We didn't have a lot of consciousness about the labor movement. We had some knowledge

Labor leader Rodolfo Robles, who has helped strengthen Guatemala's labor movement and also greatly helped the authors of this book. Photo Pat Crane

from what we read, but it was hard to find material or a text that spoke about unionism. It was very difficult at that time, and even now it's difficult.

Later on, in 1978 and 1979, I had the opportunity to work for the Coca-Cola bottling factory, which at that time was called the "Guatemalan Bottlers." The labor conflict of 1976–1978 had already passed, and I began to work just as the second phase of the conflict had begun to intensify.

The company hired sixty workers in an effort to destabilize the union. I was among that group. Once we were inside, the company informed us that the hiring contracts required that all of us join the workers' association. This wasn't the union but the solidarist association. This type of organization had not yet been tried in Guatemala; Coca-Cola was the first company to initiate the practice.

At that time, I was a participant in the university student movement. We could see the political and social situations in the country. We had an awareness of the labor movement and other popular movements. Although I still wasn't a leader, I was involved in a group called the BEO, the Organized Student Block. Later I was a member of the FERG, the Robin García Student Front.[1]

The FERG was formed after Robin García, a student leader from the secondary school movement, was assassinated. At that time I was in the university, and I began to form a support group. There was a very strong relationship between the students and the workers in those days; unfortunately, the same relationship doesn't exist now. It was very exciting to see how the two groups shared their problems and worked together in joint meetings. I got to know a lot of union leaders, and that created solidarity between the popular movements and the labor movement. These were my activities until 1978, when I sought a job in the Coca-Cola bottling plant.

In 1979 I began work there. I said earlier that the company had hired me, along with many other people, to destroy the union. Once I was inside the factory, however, I began to relate to the people in the union.

Because of our work in the student movement, we had a relationship with some of the union leaders, although the rank-and-

1. The BEO is the Bloque Estudiantil Organizado; the FERG is the Frente Estudiantil Robin García.

file union members inside the factory didn't know us. That all sixty members had been hired to create problems for the union made things very difficult at times.

Back then, the rank and file was very small. People were too terrorized to belong to the union. Within the company, one had the sense of being not in a workplace but in a barracks. There were extraordinary numbers of security personnel in the factory, people who were members of the security forces, soldiers, those whom we call *kaibiles*.[2] They all were at the service of the company.

Some of the managers in the plant were army officers. Fredy Maldonado, the production manager, besides having a degree in business was also an army officer. There was a captain there, as well as a lieutenant who was in charge of personnel, Lieutenant Francisco Javier Rodas. They were army officers, regulars in the army.

Therefore, it was very delicate working in the plant. Many people quit despite wages that were a bit higher than those paid in other workplaces. They couldn't find security or stability within the company.

I began to become more and more involved in the union but always as a rank-and-file member and not a leader. We began to form support groups for the executive committee of the union.

In 1980, problems intensified, not only in the Coca-Cola factory but also throughout the entire country. Even though a collective bargaining pact was in place, it wasn't enforced. The staff was subjected to inhumane treatment. For instance, our official workday began in the sales department at seven o'clock in the morning, but we had to arrive by six o'clock to wash the truck and prepare for the day. However, the clock didn't begin to count our working time until seven o'clock.

There was much pressure on the staff, but there was also a great crisis at the national level. Later on, right after the assassination of compañero Manuel López in April of 1980, my compañero Marlon also was assassinated. Marlon had joined Coca-Cola with my group, and he, too, became involved in the union after his hiring. Marlon was very conscious of his role as a worker, and, in spite of the fact that the company had hired him to cause problems, he

2. *Kaibiles* are the special army forces, similar to the Green Berets in the United States. They have the reputation of being the most brutal of all the security forces.

joined the union almost immediately. He was assassinated in April of 1980.

This assassination polarized the situation even more. After they killed the compañero Marlon, the personnel manager Lieutenant Francisco Javier Rodas was killed. He was a very aggressive person. Later, during the May Day demonstration, many people were kidnapped. A lot. The exact number was never known. At least two Coca-Cola workers were kidnapped, and their bodies appeared, cruelly tortured and mutilated. And many more compañeros from other unions were disappeared.

A direct confrontation broke out when the revolutionary organizations responded. There were denunciations of the kidnappings during the May Day demonstration.

By June, a very tense situation had developed. The crisis—the control of the population—had intensified. It was more exaggerated in the city.

At dawn on June 21, another compañero was assassinated, Edgar Rene Aldana. That compañero had bad luck, because he wasn't the intended victim. People don't know this—and I don't want to say the name of the other compañero who was the true target—but Edgar wasn't the one they wanted to kill. They wanted to kill one of the other union leaders.

We arrived at this conclusion because Edgar Rene Aldana physically resembled another compañero. The night Edgar was assassinated, he and this other man were working the same shift. This man was tired, and he asked Edgar to go outside to get a cylinder of gas for the loading machine. Edgar said, "I'll go but lend me your hat." So in the darkness the assassins confused Edgar for this other man. They realized it too late, while in the process of killing him. There was a witness to that assassination, but he never wanted to come forward.

Fortunately, one good leader was not assassinated; but unfortunately, another good leader was. As a result of the assassination, the leadership of the union had been reduced. The leaders asked for support from the rank and file, and we declared an immediate strike. It lasted eighteen days, I believe. We were under very heavy pressure.

Because of the assassinations and many other problems that were occurring, some leaders of the CNT, the National Workers' Central, met in the CNT headquarters to evaluate the situation. They made demands to the government that the kidnapped and disappeared be returned.

At about eleven o'clock in the morning on June 21st, the CNT was broken into and all the people attending the meeting were taken away. Included in this group were two compañeros from the Coca-Cola union. Later, these leaders were referred to as the "detained-disappeared." This was a kidnapping, but it began with a detention, with an office broken into, and a door broken down by a police car.

When a request is made that someone be presented to the court, a writ of habeus corpus must be used. We did this, and the court said, "We don't have access to them; it's a police matter." So we members of the Coca-Cola union decided to go on strike until the compañeros reappeared or were released. The company asked for police intervention; however, we were able to maintain a strike for many days. One day, two compañeros were injured when several men drove by in cars and on motorcycles shooting with machine guns into the factory. This did not intimidate us; we continued to put on the pressure.

My participation at that time was as a rank-and-file member. We carried out what the executive committee determined had to be done. The executive committee ordered us to block the entrances with trucks, to block them as much as possible with bottles.[3] We had occupied the plant.

The police came, and two more compañeros were captured. The police confronted us and said whoever didn't want to work could leave the factory. They ordered that the strike be ended. There were about two hundred heavily armed police with weapons aimed at us. It is tough to disobey an order when there are machine guns aimed at you. So factory operations were restarted, but the compañeros for whom that strike was carried out never reappeared.

As I said, my participation at that time was as a rank-and-file member. The movement in Coca-Cola is very special in that sense, because no one gets to occupy a leadership position if he or she hasn't proven a level of commitment. That's how it should be. So I spent four years as a rank-and-file member.

3. The entrances were blocked with trucks and bottles because that was all the workers had on hand to use.

Through the intervention of the IUF, a new management group took over the Coca-Cola factory. The man in charge, who was named Méndez, brought a totally new policy to the factory.[4] I can't say that these new managers were repressive, although they did have the goal of closing and decapitalizing the company.

Because of repression throughout the country, nothing was going on inside the Coca-Cola factory. Supposedly there weren't conflicts, just "domestic problems." Meanwhile, these managers were leading the company into bankruptcy. We began to realize what they were doing, and we formed a support committee for the union's directorate. With the authorization of the executive committee, we managed to disempower many people within the solidarist association who were trying to neutralize the union.

In 1982 and 1983, a serious conflict began, one that lasted for a long time. We began to take direct action, including reducing our work hours. We refused to work overtime. The union took a series of measures so that the administration would respect the collective bargaining pact that was being violated. By then, the union had affiliated with the IUF. The IUF began to pressure the company to honor the collective bargaining pact that had been established in 1980 between the union and the international Coca-Cola organization. We had to be on top of every situation to see that the contract was upheld.

So for the first time, I participated in a negotiating commission. This negotiation didn't take place in Guatemala but in Venezuela. We wanted to take advantage of the 20th Congress, I think, of the Latin American IUF, and the company was told, "When you want to resolve the problems, we are ready to negotiate. But the negotiations are going to be held in Venezuela."

The company's representatives thought they were going to be able to manipulate us, but when they arrived in Venezuela they realized that it wasn't just us, the representatives of the Coca-Cola union at the meeting, but also representatives of *all* the unions affiliated with the Latin American IUF. So they negotiated quickly; in one afternoon we came to an agreement. The union sent a telex to the compañeros back in Guatemala, and all actions were stopped.

---

4. Zash and Méndez are the men who bought out the plant after a previous labor dispute ended.

I wasn't a member of the executive committee. I was a rank-and-file member. But I was a supporting member of the negotiations. At that time I was studying to be a lawyer; however, I never finished my studies.

Later on, in mid-1983 I think, a new executive committee was elected, and the leadership proposed that I seek a place in the new directorate. I accepted the responsibility. Those of us who were elected seemed to have little in common with one another, but we soon realized that we had a great deal in common in our perspectives.

You were elected general secretary?

Yes, I was the general secretary.

We immediately had to make a work plan, knowing that the company was up to something. We had a big problem in the sense that after the Zash-Méndez administration came to Coca-Cola in 1981, they had allowed many things to happen that produced anarchy. For example, absenteeism among the workers had risen to 52 percent, which was too much. The company was allowing a great many absences from work without saying anything to the workers.

People thought that the company was respecting the union, but this was not the case. Rather, the company was creating conditions for the plant to close, to declare bankruptcy. Among other things, they were diverting the company's capital. We had suspicions about some of these maneuvers but not all of them. We saw, for example, that average daily sales were twenty thousand cases, but income was noted for only ten thousand. So at least 50 percent of the revenue was being diverted.

During this time, the rank-and-file members of the union began distancing themselves from the union. They only came to the union office when they had to resolve some type of personal problem or a work problem of little significance. They didn't take into account the fact that many people had been assassinated trying to build the union.

Not much attention was paid to this growing problem. It reached the extreme that people working in one department didn't even know the people working in another department. For example, many people who worked in sales, and who are usually in trucks on the streets, didn't know the people inside the bottling plant. Therefore, there wasn't communication among the workers. Not even as compañeros, not even as members of the union. This was very worrisome to us as the new executive committee. What were we going to do? We saw the need to design a project, a plan, to bring the people together.

We were still under a military regime, and we knew that the situation would get more serious. We had experienced another coup d'état in 1982, when Ríos Montt seized power, and people argued that because of this crisis they couldn't participate in the union struggle.

We created a project in which people would have to integrate themselves again and get to know one another. We began to develop what is currently known as the union's gym, the Plaza of Martyrs. It's a simple construction, but the significant thing is that the people built it and it serves as the sports field of the plant. The idea was that people would participate. People from different departments within the plant became involved in the project, so there was an increased level of fraternity.

In addition, we formed a support commission. We did this without people asking us to. (It was obligatory to form collective disciplinary commissions, a new method of internal organization.) There were seven people on the executive committee and three on the consulting committee, for a total of ten. We formed the support commission and a collective disciplinary commission with 154 people. These were rotating positions that changed every three months. In this way, everyone would have direct contact with the union almost all the time.

This organization helped us when the plant closed. On the night of February 17, management told us that the company was closing and that no one could stay there. But we had an emergency network in place, and by nine o'clock that night we had a hundred people inside the plant. This was the result of the work we had carried out. We had union members and union leaders struggling together. We did what could be done, and we formed a group that spent more than a year peacefully occupying the plant.

The occupation itself gave us experience for developing other types of methods for confronting conflict and the opportunity to assimilate these various methods. It also gave us the chance to develop more understanding, to relate to more people, and to see the positive nature of international relations.

I feel that I owe the little I know to the union, so I try to give all my time to my work. After the union won the struggle and the plant was reopened, I was offered the job of organizing an office for the IUF in Guatemala. That work began to blossom.

We have grown, we have developed, but not in great proportions because there aren't many of us. Our work is to support the labor movement and the popular movement in Guatemala. Each day we live through and assimilate new experiences. I consider myself a member, not a leader. The truth is that I have never considered myself to be a leader. Yet with each day that passes, one continues to accumulate understanding, and I feel satisfied and proud of the fact that I haven't retreated.

There are many valuable and capable leaders who stood out in the 1980s, but they got stuck there. These good people simply got stuck in 1980. I suppose they are still alive, but in their minds they couldn't continue to develop according to the current needs of the situation. In that sense I'm proud that year after year, apart from getting older, I am renewing myself in relation to what is happening at the international and national level.

When you began your involvement in the labor movement, did you talk with your family about your decision?

Well, no. Unfortunately, one of the biggest problems we have here in Guatemala is that the labor movement has developed within an atmosphere of such terror. I would say that 99 percent of the people who have worked at the leadership level never communicate to their family what they are doing because, logically, the family is going to say, "No, don't get involved in that because they're going to kill you. They have killed so many."

So this requires that you act in a clandestine way with regard to your family. You hide the work you do. There is no way completely to inform the family, at least until one is more involved and activities are publicly known. This is true in my case and in the case of many, many compañeros.

In 1982 and 1983, when I became very involved in the union and was elected, my family hadn't known that I was involved in union activities. When I came home late, it was supposedly because I was at the university or because I was busy with other activities.

They didn't know I was doing work for the union until I was elected.

My children didn't understand what was going on, but in the 1984 conflict they became involved. My oldest child, who is now twenty years old, and my youngest, who is now thirteen, have participated in the union through the theater group. During the occupation, they were practically living in the plant, and they learned a lot about union activity. They have developed, not a huge degree of consciousness, but an identification with the movement and with social problems.[5]

How did you respond when your compañera told you not to get involved in the struggle?

Well, it's a very difficult situation, and in general it depends on the relationship a man has with his compañera. I've been married for more than twenty years, and that creates a greater degree of understanding.

When I became involved in the union, I had been married for several years. We had a discussion, and in the end my compañera had to accept it. She realized that what I was proposing was a necessity: more freedom to participate.

The day they told us of the plant closing, my wife and my children came to the plant. They knew I was going to come home late, and they came to offer me support, to accompany me. But I told them, "Go home, it isn't safe. They might kill one of us, but we can't let them kill us all." I was not trying to be a martyr, because I don't have what it takes to be a martyr. If anyone loves life, I do. But yes, there was a clear understanding about the need to offer something to the union. Later on, when she was working for a food company, my wife contributed a lot during the occupation.

How were your children and your family affected by the occupation? You spent more than a year in the plant.

My children went to school in the morning, and in the afternoon they came to the plant. Sometimes I didn't even realize that they

---

5. Since this interview was conducted, Rodolfo Robles's oldest daughter has assumed a national leadership position in the union movement, and his son conducts support work for the UITA office.

stayed there. The girls (I have two daughters) helped out in the office. They were in the theater group, and they related to everyone. They are well known now. My son went with the salespeople, who had their tents or little houses they'd constructed in the plant. I didn't realize where they had stayed until the next day when they went to school. They had a very direct relationship with people, and this allowed them a greater degree of identification and involvement. I have many pictures of them participating in different activities, pictures taken by compañeros.

How have you personally been affected by the repression? Have you received threats?

I have said many times that in Guatemala, unfortunately, one becomes accustomed to the fact that at any moment something can happen. I'm not talking about just to myself but to any citizen. And particularly to the people involved in the popular movement.

I have received many threats. In 1986, I was kidnapped for several hours. Evidently the intention was to scare me. I must assume that was the idea, because if they had wanted to kill me they could have done so. They grabbed me in the street. I was in a car, and when I stopped at an intersection they came up and aimed guns at me. They got into the car and asked me if I was a unionist. I said, "Yes." They said, "Don't worry. We aren't going to do anything to you." "So let me go," I replied. But they didn't let me go. They drove me all over the southern part of the city. Finally they released me. It was intimidation, and it did scare me quite a bit. It had to happen sometime. Fortunately, it was just intimidation.

Later in those years, there were telephone threats. Sometimes I was followed, always with the intention of intimidating me. Thankfully, there hasn't been any more direct action. But I know there is constant surveillance of my house and the office where we work. One gets accustomed to this and considers it part of the price to be paid in this kind of work.

Not everyone becomes accustomed to it. Some people withdraw or flee the country. Why have you continued in the struggle?

Here I am going to dissent from many people who at the first signs of trouble say, "I gave enough. I'm not going to risk more. I'm fleeing the country."

I think one should analyze the situation. How likely is it that something is going to happen? How likely is it that something will happen immediately? It's difficult, very difficult, because here one never knows how the security forces are going to respond.

I don't know. I feel that I couldn't adapt to another country if I left. I feel there is too much to do here in Guatemala.

Many compañeros have left. Sometimes they left because they were the victims of some type of violence. In many cases, they barely escaped being killed. Some of their homes were machine gunned. If they were fortunate enough not to be hurt, it would be very stupid to stay.

I feel that as long as something doesn't happen, one should wait a while. Many who left got lost in the system where they now live. I know a lot of compañeros, good leaders, good activists, who have gone to the United States or to Canada or to other countries in Europe. The system absorbs them, and they don't do anything. They are immediately neutralized. So I am more afraid of being neutralized outside than inside.

Why do you think the threats have not been carried out against you?

Well, we can't say it's luck. There are many factors involved. Look at how many people they have assassinated—very well-known people. For example, Oquelí Colindres, who was assassinated despite being a very well-known politician internationally.[6]

That case notwithstanding, I believe that my constant work with people at an international level has protected me. We work within the law; we don't go outside of it. Our work is to support the labor movement, particularly to contribute something to the most economically repressed sectors. And since there has been an international response to that aspect of the work, there is permanent attention to our efforts. This has been important. It has given me some immunity and the ability to work effectively without a great

6. Hector Oquelí Colindres, a Salvadoran representative of the International Socialist Party, and Gilda Flores, a Guatemalan lawyer from the Socialist Party, were assassinated in Guatemala in January 1990. These crimes, like most others, have never been punished, despite protests from the International Socialist Party.

deal of repression or hostility. But I can't discount the possibility that suddenly I could be harassed or punished.

Have these threats and the danger affected your family?

Of course. In the case of my compañera, it has meant living under a great deal of tension. This has resulted in some illnesses. The children have not been as affected. A young person or an adolescent doesn't comprehend the danger. But their mother has been greatly affected.

On August 15th of last year, some armed men came to the house. They didn't say anything; the only thing they did was park their car in front of the door and get out with machine guns in their hands. I wasn't at home; I was in the UITA office. My family called the office to tell me that these men were outside the house and that I shouldn't come home. They asked what they should do. I told them not to go outside, and to call the police.

These things create or increase marital tensions, emotional tensions. So my compañera has been affected by nervous tensions; she has been ill.

And how is your health?

I think I've been able to create organic defense mechanisms, and despite the quantity of activities, I don't remember having been sick. It could be that in the end I'll have some fatal or grave illness. The truth is that I have doctor friends who have said to me, "Come in for a checkup, or the next time you come it will be for an autopsy." But I don't feel ill. I don't worry about that. I believe if I were to worry about that, I really would get sick!

Having seen so many compañeros fall, having seen so much repression, what motivates you to continue?

Precisely that: the repression. At times we have spoken with a compañero, and a day or two later this compañero has been disappeared or assassinated. So I think one should offer something for those compañeros. It would be a betrayal to them to stop the struggle they helped start.

I've known many people who have fallen. Fernando García, Mancy Villatoro, Julio Cermeño, compañero Alvarado—so many that I don't remember all their first and last names. All of those people have contributed to the movement. While the movement hasn't grown sufficiently, it has been maintained. It has been developing little by little because of the contributions all of these people have made.

How would it be if we withdrew from the struggle? If we withdrew out of fear? The movement would go backward and we would disperse.

So that is my motivation. The injustice. Because the level of injustice in Guatemala is horrible.

What hopes do you have for the labor movement?

Hope never dies. And as long as there is hope, there are going to be objectives to struggle for. In the workers' movement, they say as long as people are subjected to this level of injustice there will be only one option: to challenge the oppression, to change the structure completely so that people develop themselves and live in a real democracy. Such a democracy doesn't exist for us. What we have now isn't a popular democracy.

So we have to maintain hope to live, not only to live but to live *well*. To live just for the sake of living doesn't make sense.

I believe I have contributed to something important. I am making my contribution, and the people, the labor movement, and the popular movement are going to reach their objective.

What can people in the United States and Europe do to support the labor movement in Guatemala?

The important thing is that many people are unaware that Central America exists, let alone Guatemala. Many people can't say exactly where Central America is, or where Guatemala is.

To the degree that they can locate the country geographically, they can wonder about the situation of the Central American people and, in particular, the Guatemalan people. They can identify with the level of repression that the Guatemalan people suffer. We need people to understand our reality. We need to share experiences and understandings, to build an awareness of what happens in Guatemala.

Finally, I want to take advantage of this opportunity to congratulate you for doing this book and for having it published in Spanish as well as English. I have seen a lot of material about Guatemala in a number of languages but rarely in Spanish. People who have written about Guatemala have done so with good intentions; they're offering something to our country and to El Salvador, Nicaragua, and all oppressed countries. But they contribute even more if the work is published in Spanish.

Unfortunately, we're ignorant of our own roots. I told a member of the United States Congress last week that in Guatemala City people don't even know that forty kilometers away, the air force is bombing the civilian population. If people don't become aware of their own suffering, they will not be able to react.

So your work is very positive, particularly because it is going to come out in Spanish. It isn't extremely important that profits be made from this book. A huge profit would be that this material return here and that people say, "This is a portrait of me. I am that person. This is my people. That is what my people suffer." That will be a great contribution.

Selected Readings

Guatemalan History

Barry, Tom. 1990. *Guatemala: A Country Guide*. Albuquerque, N.M.: Resource Center.

Berryman, Phillip. 1984. *The Religious Roots of Rebellion: Christians in Central American Revolutions*. New York: Orbis Books.

Black, George. 1984. *Garrison Guatemala*. New York: Monthly Review Press.

Burgos-Debray, Elizabeth. 1983. *I, Rigoberta Menchu*. New York: Schocken Books.

Carmack, Robert, editor. 1988. *Harvest of Violence: The Maya Indians and the Guatemalan Crisis*. Norman: University of Oklahoma Press.

Handy, Jim. 1984. *Gift of the Devil: A History of Guatemala*. Boston: South End Press.

Jonas, Susanne. 1991. *The Battle for Guatemala: Rebels, Death Squads, and U.S. Power*. Boulder/San Francisco: Westview Press.

Manz, Beatriz. 1987. *Refugees of a Hidden War: Aftermath of Counterinsurgency in Guatemala*. Albany: SUNY Press.

Painter, James. 1987. *Guatemala: False Hope, False Freedom*. London: Latin American Bureau.

Simon, Jean Marie. 1988. *Guatemala: Eternal Spring—Eternal Tyranny*. New York: Norton.

Schlesinger, Stephen, and Stephen Kinzer. 1982. *Bitter Fruit: The Untold Story of the American Coup in Guatemala*. Garden City, N.Y.: Doubleday.

Guatemalan Labor and Peasant Movement

Albizures, Miguel Angel. 1987. *Tiempo de Sudor y Lucha*. Mexico City: Talleres de Praxis.

Alvarez, Guadalupe Navas. 1979. *El Movimiento Sindical como Manifestación de la Lucha de Clases*. Guatemala City: Editorial Universitaria, Universidad de San Carlos.

Anon. 1989. *El Movimiento Sindical en Guatemala, 1975–1985*. Mexico City: CITGUA (Ciencia y Tecnología para Guatemala).

Frundt, Henry J. 1987. *Refreshing Pauses: Coca-Cola and Human Rights in Guatemala*. New York: Praeger.

Gatehouse, Mike, and Miguel Angel Reyes. 1987. *Soft Drink/Hard Labor: Guatemalan Workers Occupy Coca-Cola*. London: Latin American Bureau.

Goldston, James A. 1989. *Shattered Hope: Guatemalan Workers and the Promise of Democracy*. Boulder/San Francisco: Westview Press.

Larrave, Mario López. 1976. *Breve Historia del Movimiento Sindical Guatemalteco*. Guatemala City: Editorial Universitaria, Universidad de San Carlos.

Levenson-Estrada, Deborah. 1994. *Trade Unionists against Terror: Guatemala City, 1954–1985*. Chapel Hill: University of North Carolina Press.

Menchu, Rigoberta, and Comité de Unidad Campesina. 1992. *Trenzando el Futuro: Luchas campesinas en la historia reciente de Guatemala*. Gipuzkoa: Tercera Prensa—Hirugarren Prentsa, S.L.

Petersen, Kurt. 1992. *The Maquiladora Revolution in Guatemala*. New Haven: Orville H. Schell, Jr. Center for International Human Rights at Yale Law School.

Sánchez, Antonio Obando. 1978. *Memorias: Historial del Movimiento Sindical Guatemalteco en Este Siglo*. Guatemala City: Editorial Universitaria, Universidad de San Carlos.

Selected Solidarity Organizations

Network in Solidarity with the People of Guatemala (NISGUA)
1500 Massachusetts Avenue, N.W., #241
Washington, DC 20005
Phone: 202-223-6474
Fax: 202-223-8221
E-mail: nisgua@igc.apc.org
NISGUA educates the U.S. public about Guatemala through speaking tours, delegations, and publications. It directly supports the popular movement in Guatemala and works to reorient U.S. policy toward Guatemala. It coordinates the efforts of more than two hundred committees and individuals in the United States and Canada.

National Coordinating Office on Refugees and the Displaced of
   Guatemala (NCOORD)
59 East Van Buren Street, Suite 1400
Chicago, IL 60605
Phone: 312-360-1705
Fax: 312-939-3272
E-mail: ncoord@igc.apc.org
NCOORD coordinates support work and accompaniment for the returning refugee population, the Communities of Population in Resistance, and the internally displaced.

U.S./Guatemala Labor Education Project (US/GLEP)
c/o ACTWU
333 South Ashland Street
Chicago, IL 60607
Phone: 312-262-6502
Fax: 312-262-6602
E-mail: usglep@igc.apc.org

US/GLEP builds solidarity between U.S. and Guatemalan unionists and organizes broad-based campaigns aimed at engendering support for internationally recognized workers' rights in Guatemala.

Peace Brigades International/USA (PBI)
2642 College Avenue
Berkeley, CA 94704
Phone/Fax: 510-540-0749
E-mail: pbiusa@igc.apc.org
PBI sponsors a team that offers accompaniment to the popular movement in Guatemala. They require a seven-month minimum commitment following completion of a training course and approval for team membership by former team members. There are also PBI-led delegations to Guatemala.

Witness for Peace (WFP)
110 Maryland Avenue N.E., Suite 311
Washington, DC 20002
Phone: 202-544-0781
Fax: 202-544-1187
E-mail: witness@igc.apc.org
WFP has a long-term team in Guatemala, which works closely with religious groups. A one-year minimum commitment is required, as is training. Witness for Peace also works to reorient U.S. policy and sponsors delegations to Guatemala.

Ecumenical Program on Central America (EPICA)
1470 Irving Street, N.W.
Washington, DC 20010
Phone: 202-332-0292
Fax: 202-332-1184
E-mail: epica@igc.apc.org
EPICA leads delegations, publishes books, and conducts support work for the refugees and the Communities of Population in Resistance. It works not only in Guatemala but also in other Central American countries.

Index